Dangerous Competition

Dangerous Competition

Critical Issues in eCompetitive
Intelligence Analysis

Richard Telofski

Writers Club Press
San Jose New York Lincoln Shanghai

Dangerous Competition
Critical Issues in eCompetitive Intelligence Analysis

Writers Club Press
an imprint of iUniverse.com, Inc.

For information address:
iUniverse.com, Inc.
5220 S 16th, Ste. 200
Lincoln, NE 68512
www.iuniverse.com

The information offered in this book is of a general nature. The information offered in this book has been obtained from sources believed to be reliable. However, the information in this book is not guaranteed to be complete or accurate. As such, the information is not intended to be, nor should it be construed as, a professional service or advice or assistance specific to any situation. The information is offered with the understanding that the author is not rendering a professional service of any type or expert assistance or advice of any kind through the information presented in this book. Thus, the author shall not be responsible for any errors or omissions or damages arising out of the use of the information in this book. For professional service, expert assistance, or specific advice, the reader should enlist the help of a qualified specialist.

ISBN: 0-595-17692-5

Printed in the United States of America

For Cally,
Who Tutored Me in My Own Humanity

CONTENTS

The Beginning 1

The Eleven Critical Concepts 21

    Space Vanquished *21*

    Size Doesn't Matter *26*

    Tempus Novo *28*

    Social, not Technical, Science *32*

    Economic Webs *35*

    Increasing Demand *38*

    Friction Elimination *40*

    Brands Moribund *42*

    Fractal Freedom *43*

    Demon Demographics *45*

    Managerial Flux *47*

The Issues 50

    Site Content & Functionality *51*

    Strategy & Mission *55*

    Marketing *86*

    Management & Organization *113*

    Financial *126*

The Finish 131

THE BEGINNING

I'll lay it on the line right now. If you think this book is a compendium of competitive intelligence sources and methods to be applied in ebusiness, then think again. It is not. A book that describes competitive intelligence methodologies and sources for application in ebusiness, at this writing, does not exist. Perhaps so with good reason.

Intelligence—The evaluated
conclusions drawn from information.

The reason is that such a book simply is not needed. That book is not needed because in ebusiness competitive intelligence we will use essentially the same sources and methods that we apply in "physical world" competitive intelligence. What differs in ebusiness competitive intelligence are the questions that we must ask in order to analyze correctly our competitive target of interest. *Dangerous Competition* identifies and discusses the special critical questions competitive intelligence analysts must ask about their ebusiness competitors before applying their methodology and hunting down sources.

In its narration, *Dangerous Competition* does occasionally suggest some competitive intelligence methods and sources which may be applied, but the book does not cover these in great detail. Why? Two reasons. First, this book is recommended for intermediate to advanced competitive intelligence practitioners who are already very knowledgeable in collection sources and methods. Second, as I already mentioned, many of the same tried and true competitive intelligence sources and collection methods applied to offline competitors may also be used to research online competition. An experienced competitive intelligence analyst will know what sources, methods, and tools, to apply to the questions reviewed in this book. But, most experienced physical world competitive intelligence analysts will not know the critical competitive issues around which ebusiness revolves. They'll have the tools, but they won't know how to apply them. So, the main difference between doing competitive research on an offline and on an online competitor is knowing for what to look. The online animal is very different. We must look for different characteristics. We must ask different questions about that different animal. It is these questions that this book explores.

Now, if you're a total novice at competitive intelligence, then don't fret. You can still benefit from this book. When I say "novice," I mean a competitive intelligence analyst who has put in less than a full year of time at the pursuit. Based on my experience, one year of work at competitive intelligence is enough to be considered an "intermediate," and plenty of time to get one's feet wet in the different methodologies and sources that exist for competitive intelligence. Novices will just need to do some simultaneous work in sources and methodologies so as to develop that "creative instinct" all analysts apply when selecting tools for the intelligence project at hand.

But, if indeed what you seek is some pronouncement of special sources and methods to be used in ebusiness competitive intelligence, then return this book. Because those types of sources and methods don't actually exist, you will be disappointed.

*　　　　　*　　　　　*

I've been in the competitive intelligence field for over twelve years. In that time, I've met a lot of smart people, but I've met many times that number of idiots. What has amazed me in this time is how competitive researchers, most of whom work for major multinational corporations, clamor to learn about new sources and methods. They practically fall all over themselves in order to learn incrementally infinitesimal nuances about sources and methods that they already know cold, so cold that they could probably write a dissertation about these sources and methods while they were asleep.

In order to convince their management that they are improving their professional skills, these individuals go to one competitive intelligence seminar after the other, listening to some windbag drone on and on about this database or that Web site or this interview method or that government document source. Ah, yes. Alas, they've heard it all before. They lament that nothing is really new. Then, after the lamenting they declare to their fellow competitive intelligerati that they already knew everything that was said in the seminars. Many of these complaints have I heard my colleagues make. Then the lamenting turns into the disparagement of the presenters. The corporate competitive intelligence personnel enter into this disparagement in such a way that their own complaints convince them of their own self-importance.

Upon return to their office, they fill out their expense report. Feelings of internal conflict arise. They've already spent a couple thousand dollars of their boss' budget, not to mention the implicit expense of their time while they were at the seminar. "Well," they think. "If it cost so much, I guess it wasn't all that bad." So, they tell their management that the seminar was "good" and because they must constantly "upgrade" their skills, they have their eye on another seminar four months hence. They ask their boss to please reserve funding for the event. The cycle is complete and set to start again in four months.

Is attendance at these sources and methods seminars intended to be a learning experience or just an excuse to get out of the office for a while? I think you know the true answer. Who should really be disparaged here? The seminar presenter or the dweebs sitting in the audience, too dumb to know that they already know what they need to know?

Does this appear to be a harsh treatment of corporate competitive intelligence types?

Too bad. You bet it's harsh. But, please don't be angry because anger is not the emotion that I am trying to elicit. What I am trying to elicit is rage, enough to shake you out of thinking within that safe little paradigm in which you have been stumbling about for the past oh so many years. I want to incense you into thinking about something different. Different. And I don't care if my approach causes you to dislike me or not. My approach and I are not the issue. What's at issue here is this new economy in which we find ourselves plunked down.

Like it or not, this new economy is different. In order to be an effective competitive intelligence analyst, and in order for the field of competitive intelligence to move beyond the stagnated position in which it presently finds itself, then you must get over it. You must absolutely be different and think about something other than sources and methods.

That something other is this. Competitive intelligence analysts need to become more astute about the "what" and less concerned with the "how." If you have been practicing competitive intelligence for a corporation, large or small, for at least a few years, then, as I have alluded, you have acquired about all the knowledge that you will need concerning "how" to look for competitive intelligence, i.e., you've learned about 90% of the critical sources and methods to use. Think about this.

Think about when you go shopping for anything. Do you have to hone your shopping skill? Do you take a course or read a book about the act of shopping in order to improve your hunting skills? Of course you don't. But, if you had to go shopping for something which you had never purchased before, you would certainly seek information about *what things* you needed to know about the novel product or service to be purchased. It's the same way in the field of competitive intelligence.

If you have been practicing for at least a few years, you've pretty much learned everything you need to know about sources and methods. You don't know every source and method, of course. But most importantly you have learned how to learn about more sources and methods and how to dig them out yourself. You've learned how to shop. Anything more you learn about sources and methods is incremental to your present skill and will likely have little contribution toward your ultimate success. Think about this, too.

As you have gone to more and more competitive intelligence seminars and have "learned" more and more about sources and methods and have spent more and more department budget, has your top management become as proportionally more interested in what value you bring to the company? I'll bet not, and the reason is probably this. Although you are expert at obtaining information, you are probably not an expert at obtaining the RIGHT information. You haven't learned about what you need to know. Or if you think you have, and senior management still doesn't respect you, then you haven't learned enough about what *they* need to know. You haven't yet hit them where they live. Because you don't know what to know about, you cannot obtain the right information and you cannot possibly produce strategic intelligence, the key to the "bottom line."

I first got involved with formalized competitive intelligence in 1989 as a strategic planning manager. In that job, I started gaining and using competitive intelligence. My focus at that time was to obtain intelligence about foreign competitors. Although foreign competitive intelligence is more difficult to obtain than domestic, after some time I became quite adept at generating the intelligence which I needed. At that time I was working for a small consulting organization. Being small, the professionals in the unit had to wear several hats. Some folks may view this as a disadvantage to the final work product. But I saw it as an advantage. I was the collector, analyst, and user of the intelligence. I knew what I needed to form a strategic plan and went after the information that would achieve that goal. I knew what was in my head.

At that time, becoming a prolific researcher was quite straightforward. Dialog, Datastar, Genie, and Prodigy made it all quite simple, generating reams of information and data to be processed into intelligence. Today, with even more and better information providers, it is even easier. With the explosion of the World Wide Web, in these days of information over-load, the competitive intelligence analyst has no problem in retrieving and generating information.

Info Overload—Too much
generality and not enough specificity

There is plenty to be had. It is simple to obtain. And much of it is inexpensive. The real problem for the analyst is identifying what is important and then making sense of what is obtained. In order to be able to identify what information is important, and then to make sense of and make action with that information, the competitive intelligence analyst must have an understanding of the way a company is organized and how it functions in the analyst's particular industry. Elements of strategy are a prerequisite understanding in intelligence analysis.

In my tenure as a competitive intelligence analyst, I have met many corporate competitive intelligence managers who are expert at intelligence retrieval, but only a few who are expert at analysis. Why? My opinion is that it is the fault of their management. Too many of their management saw and see the competitive intelligence process as information retrieval when what they really want is analysis. Consequently, management hired many librarian types to do the work. I can't tell you how many competitive intelligence "analysts" I have met with library science degrees. Now, there is nothing inherently wrong with librarians in these jobs. Some of my best friends have been librarians, especially on a desperate trip to my college library the night before a paper was due. But a problem, a major problem, arises through staffing the competitive intelligence function with librarians or pure information retrievers. We get people who are not well grounded in the process of business management and strategy, either through schooling or through experience or both. Even though I may have wished otherwise, just as that late night librarian wasn't there to write my paper, the corporate information retriever is not there to analyze, although analysis may be just what management, in its heart of hearts, wants. Thus, a disconnect arises. A disconnect between what management expects and what it sets itself up to get.

In order to make sense of the information and to form it into intelligence, one must understand the environment from which the information arrives. Imagine that you are playing football, a linebacker on a defensive team. If you do not know how to play the game, then the signals that you hear coming from the opposing quarterback will be meaningless. You won't have any indication of what the number 2 in the called audible 32 means. And while you're standing there trying to figure it out, the center will snap the ball and you, my friend, are going to get run over by a big, burly, hairy, knuckle-dragging, 250 pound, pulling guard from Michigan named "Tiny."

The problem with librarians doing competitive intelligence is that they are like the football team manager. They organize everything from being told what to do by the coach. But they often don't do the right things at the right times. Why? Because they have never actually played the game, they don't operate on gut feel, they don't know what is in the head of the coach or the players. So, they muddle through, doing the best that they can. Is it the team manager's fault that he/she is not instinctively responsive? Should the coach chastise the team manager when the right play book page is not handed to him/her at the proper moment? Not necessarily. It's not entirely the fault of the team manager. It's largely the fault of the coach who selected this particular team manager. The coach selected a manager who doesn't have the game in his or her head.

In business, understanding that game means having a good foundation in business strategy, knowing competitive strengths and weaknesses and how the competitor positions those strengths and weaknesses to advantage. When competitive intelligence personnel don't have this foundation, corporate competitive intelligence managers have a difficult time in making their case to corporate management, who are constantly jockeying thoughts of internal and external strategies in their minds. In other words, the competitive intelligence personnel don't know what's in management's head.

To make up for this lack of understanding, they bury their clients, i.e., corporate management, in a sea of information, which they like to call intelligence. But we really know that it is not actually intelligence. Intelligence is analyzed information, with logical conclusions about external business strategies drawn from it. If the competitive intelligence folks don't understand strategy, they can't analyze information into forward-looking intelligence. No matter how competitive intelligence folks dress it up, their product just becomes information. Management is already overwhelmed with information, which is what they see it as, not the actionable intelligence they crave. So, why doesn't management get from the competitive intelligence analyst the intelligence that they crave? Because, say it with me:

The analyst doesn't know what's in management's head.

So what is happening here is that management is perpetuating its own problem in a vicious circle. Management sees the competitive intelligence function as largely information gathering because that is what they have always received from the competitive intelligence folks. Management therefore hires information retrievers for competitive intelligence positions, not analysts, even though they may call them analysts. The analysts, because they are retrievers and don't have the proper background in strategy, give management information, but call it intelligence. And so on. I've seen this happen so many times, that corporate management loses faith in the intelligence function, laying off the competitive intelligence personnel and abolishing the competitive intelligence positions. Management loses a vital function because of its own inability to truly understand the nature of the competitive intelligence function and the types of persons who must occupy those positions.

The competitive intelligence analyst has got to realize another simple truth as well. Corporate managers are highly risk averse.

In 25 years of business, I have yet to meet one corporate manager who would really stick its own neck out on a given issue. I'm sure that they're out there somewhere, though. It's just that I haven't met them yet. This risk averse behavior is supported by the very structure of a large corporation which encourages group decision making, ostensibly to benefit from the knowledge in many minds, but in actuality encouraging "group think," causing no one to take a risk. But look at it this way. If they weren't risk averse, they wouldn't be corporate managers. They'd be entrepreneurs. Or mountain climbers.

Because of this risk averse nature, corporate managers want something that will help them deflect attention from their decisions should something go south. They want something that will make their lives easier, less complicated, less risky, and that will afford them the opportunity to shift the blame to someone if the "decisions made" turn out to be questionable or worse. That something can be intelligence, i.e., conclusions drawn from information recommending specific actions.

People, competitive intelligence analysts, who give them this something will become the friends of upper management.

Eventually, in order to become the friend of upper management, if indeed that is actually one of your goals and you like being an assumer of risk, you, the corporate competitive intelligence manager or analyst, must first obtain a mastery of, or at least a vast familiarity with, business strategy in the industry in which you are employed. Obtaining such knowledge has been readily available in business school or in adult education courses. Even reading books on one's own is preferable to having little to no knowledge in this crucial field. Before undertaking such learning, though, there is one thing that must be said. Many, if not most or all, of these business strategy resources are oriented toward old line manufacturing businesses.

I obtained my MBA the way many people do, the long way, at night, part-time. I started in 1983 and graduated in 1988. Almost all of my courses were designed to give me skills and aptitude for managing a manufacturing business. This manufacturing bias was somewhat confusing to my classmates and me because, as business students, we were aware that the majority of American economic output had been in services, not manufacturing, since 1953. We raised that question with more than one professor.

"Hey, what's with the manufacturing bias? Why can't we get a little instruction on service company management?"

—*Rider College Graduate School of*
Business Administration Students, 1985

The professor, knowing we were right, would usually offer a sheepish explanation that the principles and concepts being taught could easily be abstracted to service companies. That was usually the extent of the explanation. They never offered to explain that abstraction process. My guess is that they probably didn't know how to perform such an abstraction themselves. Why? One reason could be that many of them didn't have practical management experience. They were pure academics. They had never actually played the game.

It's my understanding, however, that since I graduated many MBA programs have adopted some curricula more oriented toward service providing industries. Whew! Just in time, too. It's only been about a half century since America became a service economy. Now that they're getting comfortable with the service orientation, they'll need to change again. That change will need to be to something not quite all manufacturing, not quite all service, not even quite all physical.

Remember that video, "Let's Get Physical" with Olivia Newton-John bouncing around in a leotard? If you're older than a Generation Xer, you probably do. Well, getting physical is now less important than it once was. What about the propagation of the species you say? No, not that kind of physical. The physical nature of business is becoming less important to success. Those manufacturing, and now service, company management techniques that they teach in business education programs and books are getting new cousins because managers now need to focus on a new dimension which complicates the status quo. That new dimension, which should come as no surprise to anyone who has listened to the news during the past three years, is the virtual. In business, we call this virtuality "ebusiness."

So that the competitive intelligence analyst can know as closely as possible what is in the head of their risk averse management, when acquiring the skill of understanding business strategy they should be mindful not to settle solely on resources which are oriented toward teaching strategy concerning physical world businesses. Notice I say "solely." Certainly understanding physical world business strategy is important. It will continue to be important for many years to come, albeit at a decreasing rate. What will be important at an increasing rate, however, is the understanding of business strategy in the virtual world, the world of ebusiness.

It is to that understanding for the competitive intelligence professional that this book is directed.

eBusiness, or electronic business, is something about which we've all heard, but relatively few of us so far actually understand. eBusiness, quite plainly explained, is the process of commerce conducted via an electronic network. What we don't understand is how ebusiness will affect our companies and how ebusiness will affect our daily affairs both now and in the future.

The intent of this book is to get you to think about some ebusiness strategic issues for the competitive intelligence analyst. Through this process it is hoped that the analyst will be better able to know what is in the head of its management when it comes to dealing with ebusiness strategies and the intelligence that can reveal them. By knowing better what's in management's heads, the competitive intelligence analyst will be able to pursue the "right" information about ebusiness competitors and will be able to analyze it, turning it into risk-reducing intelligence for management, possibly becoming a friend in the process.

Now. How do I, a competitive intelligence analyst myself, know the right issues about which to ask when analyzing an ebusiness competitor? I just got finished telling you that the librarian and the football team manager are often lost because they don't have any practical, in-the-trench experience. Well, that's where I'm different. I've been in the trenches.

I left my strategic planning job in 1991 to start my own competitive intelligence consultancy. I did pretty well, too. In 1998, I put the consultancy on hold because I just had to try something else. The lure was too strong. The lure was called ebusiness. From 1998 through early 2000, I spent most of my time running several niche portal sites. These niche portals, accessed via the World Wide Web, offered information and links to vital resources desired by competitive intelligence analysts and market researchers. Being a for-profit business and not an altruistic venture, the portals were advertising supported and made money until late 1999. That's when the market for Internet advertising rates went down the crapper. Too much inventory chasing too few advertisers crashed the rates. The portals then became financially unattractive. I moved out of that business and back to my first love, competitive intelligence.

While I was "off the reservation" I learned a lot of things about ebusiness. Some of those things I learned in books, but most of them I learned in the "Internet College of Business Knowledge." This college is actually a part of the same university that my father attended, "The University of Hard Knocks." Guess what? I think I've earned my stripes. I've done competitive intelligence analysis, lots of it. I've run an ebusiness. There aren't many people who have done both. I think that I'm qualified to discuss intelligently issues in ebusiness strategy so that when you do your competitive analysis on an ebusiness competitor you can determine the special, critical questions that you as a competitive intelligence analyst need to ask.

Again, the intent of this book is to get you to think about some ebusiness strategic issues, as they relate to a company's strengths and weaknesses, for use by the competitive intelligence analyst. The book intends to accomplish this by doing two things. First, *Dangerous Competition* will discuss eleven general concepts critical to conducting business in a virtual environment. You may call it cyberspace, ebusiness, virtual business, the

Internet space, the ether world, heaven, hell, no-persons land, the Bronx, or whatever you like. But in this book conducting business virtually will be known as "ebusiness." The discussion of these general concepts critical to ebusiness is important because they form the basis of all strategy created in ebusiness. Second, this book intends to identify for competitive intelligence managers, in companies virtual and physical, some issues critical to the success of an ebusiness competitor's operation, i.e., the potential and salient strengths and weaknesses of that "ecompetitor." The book demonstrates through a question format not only what those strengths and weaknesses could be, but also why they are important, and how the competition's mastery or bungling of those factors can make that ebusiness competitor dangerous or not dangerous to your company. All of those elements will be directly related to the eleven critical concepts discussed in this book.

eBusiness is a new area of commerce. It's a new kind of animal, the behavior of which must be understood or we'll suffer the consequences. We, as competitive intelligence analysts, have that imperative. eBusiness carries with it lethal tools, ones that can make for dangerous competition. eBusiness also carries with it many traps that if not realized can ensnare their owner. The competitive intelligence analyst must adequately comprehend these issues so that proper analysis is affected, with intelligence and strategic recommendations forwarded to upper management. The dawn of this new era, which some call the "New Economy," presents an opportunity.

That opportunity is the chance for competitive intelligence analysts to excel in a critical area of business management. Because this is such a new area, many senior managers do not have an adequate understanding of the way the game is played. Think that's not true? Okay. How many times have your heard ebusiness executives interviewed on television or radio, or quoted in the press, saying that they were doing such and such just so they could try to figure out how ebusiness works? If competitive intelligence personnel can gain this vital insight first, they will lead the pack. They will not only provide risk averse upper management with the answers to what is in their heads, but also they will provide more of what should be in those managers' heads, gaining a new respect for not only themselves specifically, but also for the field of competitive intelligence in general.

*   *   *

One of the jobs of the competitive intelligence analyst is to keep his/her eye on the changes in competitors' strategies. Doing so in this New Economy, this new digital battleground we've got going, is not quite as easy as monitoring strategies in the "Old Economy," where "brick & mortar" reign supreme.

Not only were elements of strategy different in that dusty Old Economy where manufacturing and physical assets were the basis of everything, company strategies generally applied for anywhere from three to five years. Management changed those strategies slowly, with careful deliberation and pause. Or, at least we hope it was with careful deliberation and pause. There are two reasons why those industrial strategies changed so slowly. One, strategies changed slowly because they were based on hard assets, factories, matter, brick & mortar. Time was required to change the alignment of any assets in this class. You just can't redesign a factory overnight, although its been tried. Remember from economics class? All resources are variable, but only in the long run? Two, because industrial technology, before digitization, changed slowly, there just were relatively few accelerating changes in manufacturing approaches. Yes, over the past fifty years there has been much advancement in manufacturing technique, but the modern advancement pales by comparison to the level of change that took place when the Industrial Revolution began in the early 19th century.

"Change is inevitable, except from vending machines."
—*Anonymous*

The lack of remarkable advancement in the industrial world of late is because resources have been devoted to fomenting another revolution, the coming of the post-industrial era, the computer age, the information age. Pick your own moniker, this revolution is and will be televised.

We find ourselves at the beginning of this new revolution, what Alvin Toffler called the "The Third Wave." The first being agriculture, the second being industrialism, the third being the information driven economy enabled through computers. We don't know how long this revolution will last or when the breakneck pace of change will subside. But, regarding competitive intelligence and its practice, we do know this. In the New Economy, where digitization increases the pace of business transaction, strategies are valid for a much shorter period of time, perhaps twelve to eighteen months at most. Why this time period? Because according to Moore's Law technology doubles at least every 18 months. We'll talk more about Moore's law later. For right now, realize that this pace compounds the task of competitive intelligence analysts, requiring that assessments of "ecompetitors" and their strategies be accomplished more frequently and within a shorter time frame.

The driving force behind these rapidly changing strategies? As I hinted above, it's the technology, stupid.

In the Old Economy, i.e., business before the Internet, technology was empowering, the application of a new technology allowed the competitor to achieve new goals. But keep in mind this. That new technology, which usually involved computing power, was standalone. It wasn't linked to anything or anyone outside the location of where it was placed. Its growth was inhibited, but it wasn't eliminated. Advances in computing technology were continually applied to business. And when the Internet was thrown into the mix and embraced by business, the whole thing just took off and increased the revolution that was already underway. Why? Because the computing power could communicate, multiplying the amount of information we would get and from which we could learn, exponentially.

We'll discuss these important concepts in more detail later in this book. For now, let's realize this.

Today, our technology should also be regarded as empowering, but to a greater degree than ever before. Technology at its most current, always, gives us a wider selection of alternatives. When that vast array of alternatives is reviewed and the best are selected and employed, the outcome of the selection often yields disorder, a change in the status quo, a disturbance. But disturbance is not always bad. Yes, it's generally bad when a bad boy disrupts a grade school class, unless he's doing so because there's a fire in the coat room and he sees a better way of spending the afternoon than experiencing smoke inhalation. Disorder is good when it makes us see new ways of doing business and doing that business more profitably. And that's exactly what's happening today.

This disruption, hatched by infotech advances, Toffler's Third Wave, causes humans, a curious lot to begin with, to ask questions about how business can be done better, how waste can be minimized, increasing profitability. The human mind realizes that the technology can be, as it has been since the discovery of the wheel, substituted for human labor. In so doing, we can surrogate various pieces of a company's value chain. As technology advances and grows upon itself, the continual substitution of improving technology in the value chain causes strategies and supporting tactics to be reformed, at interval, continually, so that new opportunities may be exploited.

Value Chain—The steps and
processes needed to
achieve customer satisfaction.

The changes become so rapid that each technological plateau reached, and the new paradigms it supports, would be unrecognizable to persons just a generation prior.

Gordon Moore, one of the founders of Intel and presently an Internet venture capitalist, is credited with a law that says the capability of technology doubles every 18 months or the cost of technology decreases by half every 18 months. Whichever way you look at it, the law, if obeyed, will support the proliferation of more and more computing and computing related technology into the business arena, with all of the value chain and strategic changes implied. Given Moore's Law, the competitive intelligence analyst is tasked with the daunting responsibility of keeping an eye on the competition's strategy, one which will likely change, frequently and rapidly.

To get a gross indication of what those changes in competitive strategy might be, means that the competitive intelligence analyst must attend to general changes in technology, anticipating what technology will be available and applicable to the competition's operation within the next 12 to 18 months. You're not a techy? From my experience I would say that only a small proportion of competitive intelligence analysts are. Looking for these gross indicators, successfully, does not require a technical background. What is required is the skill to monitor technological developments with an interested layperson's perspective, delving deeper into available information along with the humility to ask questions when necessary. What is required is the faculty to anticipate future applications of that technology, through the development of an imaginative and creative mind. And what is most required is the business acumen to understand how those applications can be applied to strategic advantage, making your competitor's business a success.

Through the exercise of these skills, the competitive intelligence analyst can do things that no other businessperson can do. Among those things is the ability to predict, with some degree of accuracy, what an ebusiness will do, how they will do it, why they will do it, and how successful they will be at it. True competitive intelligence analysts are dedicated to digging out the facts about a business, putting them together, and making a picture that indicates a position of strength or weakness.

As the NASDAQ crashed in April 2000, I read a plethora of articles in the trade press about how this ebusiness or that ebusiness was strapped for cash. I read even more articles about how various ebusiness business models weren't working. I read about many ebusinesses that didn't have ancillary funding, couldn't find it, weren't likely to get it, and were doomed unless they could get some. Blah, blah, and yet more blah. These comments were usually not made by the journalists writing the articles. Oh, no. Internet industry analysts at world famous New Economy research companies made these comments almost exclusively. The conclusions reached by these commenting "analysts?" Their critiques concluded by saying something akin to the fact that they didn't know how much longer the ebusinesses of their particular analyses would be able to remain in business. Oh, come on. Talk about corporate wonks not wanting to stick their necks out. I thought that if I read this sort of drivel posing for competitive analysis one more time, I'd plotz.

Hey, guess what? If they did some true competitive analysis, they would be able to say, and with some degree of certainty, about how long these ebusinesses would be able to remain afloat. But let's be fair. The analysts at these world famous business research companies are often not competitive analysts. They are frequently market analysts, taking the general view, not getting into the nitty gritty to make a specific prediction. Why? They are trying to appeal to a broad audience, an audience that will buy their syndicated market research, not competitive analysis, reports. And that's OK, they have to make a living, just like anyone.

But a well-seasoned corporate competitive intelligence analyst is not so restricted. They have a more narrow and captive audience. They can, should, and are expected to get down into the nitty gritty. Through the material in this book, the competitive intelligence analyst can get help in identifying just what issues to get nitty gritty about when it comes to analyzing an ebusiness. From this book they can get help in performing a task that most world famous business analysts find elusive, i.e., determining the life expectancy of an ebusiness.

Be careful. Don't fall into the trap that has claimed so many before you. The foregoing should not be interpreted to mean that you should be wholly parochial and examine only strategies or emerging strategies for ebusiness efforts. Don't get lost in the trees looking for the forest. eBusiness does have special issues and concepts which we all need to learn and master. This book will move you toward that goal. But overall, ebusiness is still a subset of business in general. And as with any subset, it is ideally designed to work within its larger system, the one which spawned it, the one which brought it to the dance. By this I mean that ebusiness is ultimately destined to work within physical business, within the so-called Old Economy.

At some point, and I feel that point will be before the end of 2004, businesspeople will no longer promote or recognize a distinction between the "old" and "new" economies. This change will cause that ubiquitous "e" appearing in front of every word from books to hot dogs not to go away mad, but just to go away. Yes. It's true. I do use, quite liberally in fact, those "e"s in this book. So, am I hypocritical? No. At least I hope I am not. I use the "e" because at this writing the distinction still exists in far too many business minds. The employment of the "e" helps me identify and separate from physical business concepts and rules the new concepts and rules which you so desperately need to learn. After learning these new concepts and rules, you may then move on to the time when commerce will be just commerce, offline as well as online. eBusiness will be accepted as much as any form of exchange, and we won't recognize any difference. At that time, these new concepts and rules will be so engrained, that you won't likely remember that you learned them separately from the physical business concepts and rules.

So, to be an effective competitive intelligence analyst, you should adopt this view now. Do not look at your competitor's ebusiness effort in a vacuum. Realize that the ebusiness effort will impact the offline effort and vice versa. Although, the online effort will be moving and changing more quickly than the offline effort, at some future point those two efforts will merge and together they may both move more rapidly than the online effort did alone.

Okay. We're now getting closer to looking at the specific issues about which you should understand as you study your ecompetitor. But before we get there, you'll need a little priming on how ebusiness differs from its physical ancestors. To do that, let's look at the following eleven concepts.

THE ELEVEN CRITICAL CONCEPTS

Space Vanquished

You've heard the expression; "It's a small world." For business on our planet-wide village, the world is getting smaller and so is the space that makes up the world. Companies are bridging the space gaps everyday, closing the distance, sealing the deal, bringing us closer. So that's why you feel so crowded!

In the 1960s, Marshall Mc Luhan (You know, the medium is the "massage" guy? He was an anthropologist by trade, although his doctorate was in English literature.) wrote *War and Peace in the Global Village*. Mc Luhan was a very complicated theorist. In my experience it seems that many, what I mean to say is most, people don't understand him. But what he wrote about in *Global Village* was fairly easy to grasp. He wrote of how the television connected us across great distances and the effects therefrom. After Telstar was booted into orbit, almost any message could be flashed to the other side of the planet, instantly, making us all part of a global village, at least theoretically.

> *Telstar—The first of a long series*
> *of communications satellites*
> *launched in the early 1960s.*

I say theoretically because in a village there is give and take, this and that, back and forth, up and down, discourse, what we like to call interactivity. There is a conversation, having at minimum two sides. Mc Luhan's idea of a global village was somewhat different. It was unidimensional. One way. Television was then, and still mostly is now, a one way street. This unidimensionality of television is valid if you don't count Web TV or other interactive television systems which are few and far between.

In television and other conventional mass media, once the message has been received, there is little opportunity for the receiver to respond to the sender in order to modify future messages, as is done in a real village or hamlet or pueblo or town with face-to-face contact. Of course, responses may be made by letter or telephone or email or petition. But let's be real. Responding in this fashion simply is not convenient. People are busy enough as it is and if you ask them to go out of their way to make a response, then just forget about it. The response doesn't happen. We'll talk more about this idea of time possession later. It's an important one. What's really needed to make that response more likely to happen is a facility to make it more convenient. Yes. I know what you're thinking. You're thinking Internet.

But, when Mc Luhan espoused his global village theory, the Internet was only just being cobbled together. The network was originated by an American government agency called the Advanced Research Project Administration or ARPA for short. What was to eventually become the Internet was at the outset known as Arpanet, to be used by a handful of mainframe computers so that their massive computing power could be accessed in different regions of the United States in case less than all of those computers were vaporized in a nuclear tussle. If they were all vaporized, well then I guess that the Arpanet was to be only so much cabling and wire. By the time Mc Luhan died in 1980, the Internet didn't look much different than the Arpanet of the 1960s, so he never really got to experience that which could have fulfilled his theory. But even though the Internet of 1980 wasn't much different from the Arpanet of the 1960s, that network was ultimately working toward the reduction of space in our lives. Space as a barrier to interactivity, that is.

Now, of course, we have all been told over and over, ad infinitum, ad nauseum, how the Internet reduces space. Distance is vanishing. What's important for our discussion here is that the Internet is decreasing the historical position of geographical proximity as the determinant of one's competitors in business.[1]

The problem with distance in business is that it adds cost. In order to expand market coverage and compete effectively, companies had to establish physical intermediaries to reach markets that were distant to the producer. This necessity was the same for manufacturers and service companies alike. The recognition of this problem gave rise to a solution in the form of distributors for manufacturers and almost all of the fast food joints that now dot the globe.

For manufacturers, distributors became a problem solution when cheap and rapid bulk transportation became a reality. In other words, when the railroad, a type of network, became common place in various parts of the world, distributors became a viable solution to the space barrier that impeded manufacturers' progress. The establishment and supply of these far reaching distributors threatened smaller local manufacturing companies through their inability to match prices due to the distant manufacturer's economies of scale and ability to mitigate distance through cheap, bulk transportation rates.

The Internet really, in a competitive sense, is not fundamentally different from the railroad example above, except that the Internet is now used to threaten those distributors who originally knocked out the local manufacturers in markets distant. As I'm sure that you have heard, the Internet threatens the established intermediaries, whose primary job is to represent a product or service in markets physically far from the producer, through disintermediation. According to consultants Phil Evans and Tom Wurster, disintermediation, which is the eradication of an intermediary, opposite to the railroad example above, is not new and has been going on for a long time.[2] Although the railroad example was one of intermediation, the effect was the same as that of disintermediation, a changing of the established system.

The change spawned by the Internet brings buyers closer to the sellers or vice versa, not physically of course but virtually and cheaply. That's just for the interactive part of the deal. The condition that was satisfied by the distributor being local was that it facilitated face-to-face communication. Now, instead of communication having to be face-to-face, the Internet supplants that part of the value chain and supports two-way communication, interactivity, simulating virtual face-to-face contact. Not of the quality of face-to-face human interaction, but good enough to close the sale in many types of transactions. The other part of the deal, which used to be shipped on a railroad, i.e., the physical presentment of the product, can still be done and in such a way as to minimize the cost of the transaction.

Thus, in business the Internet changes the physical nature of business, the result of which is that we can actually get a more intimate global village, a virtual planetary hamlet. Commerce-wise. Market access increases, to the max.

How does a competitor leverage this new, and dangerous for you, reality?

Per writer Kevin Kelly, the central thrust of the Internet is that of communication.[3] But it is not just about communication by itself. Communication is a nice process, but in business, unless there is a point to it, everyone will go hungry. For the ebusiness competitor, the critical aspect is about communications to and from its customers to make, according to consultant Patricia Seybold, their lives easier and to save them time.[4] Not a bad idea, no matter who thought of it first.

What we're talking about here is the ability, the power, the advantage of a company, your competitor, to communicate to a mass audience or to a single individual at once, anywhere on this planet. It's a powerful competitive capability, one not to be taken lightly. "So what," you say? "TV does that!"

Ah, but remember Mc Luhan's theory. Television is effectively a one way deal. Before Mc Luhan starting saying cool stuff like, "The medium is the massage."[5] He was saying more cerebral stuff like, "The medium is the message."[6] Without a long tutorial on Mc Luhan, which could take at least 100 pages, let's just say simply that either expression means the same thing. Either expression means that the recipient is being affected by the medium itself and not necessarily the content being carried by the medium. So what this means is that Mc Luhan, as a theorist, thought mostly of the medium affecting the recipient, not the other way around.

Unlike television, radio, newspapers, and other conventional media, the Internet allows messages to go in reverse. That is to say messages, in this case content, may travel easily from your competitor's customers to your competitor. From a traditional view, we would call this "reverse" communication. This reverse communication is traditionally called feedback. But if the competitor organizes it properly and employs it properly, the reverse communications may be called market research, advice, recommendations, market intelligence, or we could even call it by a trendier term, relationships.

Call this reverse communication by any name you like. The result remains the same. The reverse communication, coming essentially from anywhere on the planet, gives the ecompetitor an opportunity to learn about what motivates a potential customer. That information may be segmented so conclusions can be drawn about different types of customers and their needs. Basic marketing this is, but on hyperdrive. And that's the basis of business, the satisfaction of need. That's a principle from the Old Economy and it won't ever be changed by the New Economy, only facilitated.

Companies are now realizing this possibility, running into the fray, some a bit too wildly if you ask me, in an attempt to make their Internet presence interactive. Your competitors, if they are smart, will realize this too and move to leverage this new reality. In so doing, they will facilitate learning from their customers, which just so happen to be the same customers that you want.

The following idea is loosely related to the issue of space problem mitigation in that communication, virtual personal communication, closes the gap. Related to the idea of interactive communication is the concept of customization. Your ecompetitors, if they're smart, can amplify the interactivity and let customers choose from a variety of customization options so that any need or want may be satisfied. Your job, as a competitive intelligence analyst, must be to study the selections offered by your ecompetitor. Study them over time. See what ones stay and what ones go. And from those changes, per consultants Stan Davis & Christopher Meyer as well as others, anticipate what customers will request next.[7] We'll talk more about this idea later.

*   *   *

Size Doesn't Matter

Competitors no longer necessarily display strength by bulking up on things like factories, warehouses, trucks, and machines. In fact, in the New Economy, these things may be regarded as liabilities, rather than as assets. Now the most powerful asset to be played is information.

Face it, Bub. The processing of information is simply more cost-effective than the processing of tangible products.[8] In processing and distributing information are cost-savings, no inventory carrying charges, no pesky unionized warehouse workers, no utility bill to choke a horse. All these things, and more, decrease the cost curve of information relative to physical products. When your ecompetitor processes and distributes information, their marginal cost approaches zero.

> *Marginal Cost—The extra cost*
> *of producing one more unit of output.*

But on the other side of the street, the revenue side, the ecompetitor's marginal revenue is at whatever price that they can set for their informational product. Guess what this situation does to their marginal profit?

"OK," you say. "This is fine for those who sell information or other products that can be jammed through a wire onto the Internet. But, what about the competitor that sells widgets?"

It's true that a widget (that favorite business school product) cannot be distributed directly through the Internet. That widget's simply too big. Physics would have to change before we could jam a widget through a wire and send it to a customer. Just imagine ordering a pair of shoes over the Web and having them pop out from your printer. Yet, we can abstract the widget. What the widget ultimately achieves can be communicated, virtually, through the Internet.

The widget, like any product or service, solves a customer problem. Duh! That is what it ultimately achieves. If any product or service does not solve a problem, its seller can remain in business only until a majority of its target market realizes their problem is not being solved.

Before a customer can solve a problem, he or she needs what? Say it with me!

>>>> *Information.*

Information, about the product or service to be used in solving their problem. The information, listing beneficial attributes, acts as a model of the product or service representing the ability of your ecompetitor's offering to solve the customer's problem. When this type of information is distributed via the Internet, with the Internet's ability to facilitate interaction, it is almost (virtually) like distributing the product itself. After all, what is a product or service other than a collection of attributes to solve a problem?

Your ecompetitor might also be distributing more of an "offering." (We'll talk more about the concept of an "offering" later.) This means paying attention to more than just the **core** product or service which is purveyed. The presence of an offering along with the communication of attributes means the competitor is attending to the customer's needs outside the core. By this I specifically mean that the competitor may let the customer help him/herself if that's what the customer wants. This service aspect may let the customer not only get information on the core offering, but may also let them perform the transaction online, change orders, adjust delivery time, check on order status online, or reconcile billing problems, which should not arise if the system is set up correctly. (We'll talk more about this later, too.) This type of electronic facility beats having the customer phone in to say:

"Hullo, I'm trying to find out if…"

for the ecompetitor and the customer, and definitely not for you.

Hullo—A colloquial
greeting generally substituted for the word "Hello."
Often uttered by people from Indiana.

So, in considering the concept of matter in business, what we have is an ecompetitor that distributes "virtual" widgets that help it close the sale of the physical widgets. We have an ecompetitor with a competitive marginal cost for the physical product which is not zero, of course, but it is greatly reduced relative to what it would have been had the ecompetitor not been able to distribute that virtual product. We also have an ecompetitor that can combine a product with service to form an offering.

This ability, to reduce a product to an informational state, or the ability to "informationalize[SM]," along with the merging of self-service, are critical and dangerous weapons in the New Economy arsenal and combined are one of the primary differentiates from the Old Economy.

*   *   *

Tempus Novo

Time. Do you feel like YOU have less of it? Are you jonesing for more?

Let's recall a simpler time, way back there in the early 1980s, just when personal computers were starting to break into the collective consciousness.

> *Jonesing—A craving, a desire, a very strong need, almost an addiction.*

We were told by they (that sociological other) that having a personal computer would make our work and/or personal lives so much more easy that we would have a lot more extra time. So where is it? I was promised extra time, but I don't see it.

Even though we have computers that are supposed to save us time, we instead feel like we don't have as much of it as these timesaving devices promised us. Why? Because that is the paradox of the age in which we live. (Sorry, that was just a cool and pretentious line that I wanted to throw in for fun.) No, the real reason is this. We're blessed and cursed at the same time. The cause of this paradox is the computer.

The computer itself makes us so much more efficient. It helps us to organize and to be more productive, saving time. If you are reading this book, then the chances are that I don't need to go on and on about the value of computers. You already know that. But what you may not realize is the trouble that they cause you. That trouble began when someone got out of bed one morning and said, "Hey! Today I think it would be great if I started to link all the time saving boxes in the world together. Wouldn't that be a hoot?" And as we saw earlier in this book, that bright idea began with Arpanet.

Once a myriad of computers became connected to the Internet, and once it was made easy for new computers to become connected, our economy became hyperconnected, more intertwined than ever before, starting a different kind of human headache than ever before. Commerce began to ebb and flow on the responses computers made to each other via the Internet. So, outside of the crashes and other piddly things that these computers make us take care of, a connected economy allows us to live in a world where responses may be made at once. That's the blessing. The curse is that because responses may be made immediately, they are therefore expected immediately. If you can, you must. There is no choice.

The more we have of something, the more people (such as customers) expect us to use it. This ability to respond immediately brings with it responsibilities. Among those responsibilities is the expectation by customers that you will satisfy at least their informational requests immediately and their product fulfillment requests very soon thereafter. Achieving this can be a formidable task. The ecompetitor who can meet the expectations of real time will be a dangerous foe, indeed.

But this responsibility also brings with it an opportunity. That is the opportunity to learn and change quickly. What this means is that in our increasingly connected state, we can anticipate, improvise, adapt, overcome.[9] Semper Fi.

The expectation of immediate response can work both ways. The customer wants an immediate response from the company. Because of this desire, the company can pretty much expect an immediate response back from the customer. After all, the customer is the impatient one, right? Remember interactivity? In this manner, ecompetitors can gain market intelligence, in much less time than previously required, and usually at a lower cost to boot.

Learning through that customer feedback is a very competitive way to monitor the development of customer needs and wants. Is your ecompetitor among these successful companies?

These companies watch the signals and then fill those changing customer needs more quickly than the competition. Could that competition be you?

Customers, being a pesky and finicky lot, will display "small windows of satisfaction opportunity." Those windows will open, close, and just generally change position. To hit those window openings correctly the successful company must be there with the right offering, at the right time. To achieve that goal, the successful company must stay connected and live on the immediate feedback gained from customers, all of which is augmented through an ebusiness process.

But please remember this, Bucko. If you feel like you have less time, then guess what?

Answer: Most other people feel the same way.

Those are the same people who you want for *YOUR* customers, and so does your ecompetitor. The attention of those potential customers will be short, real short, too short. So the successful company must give something great in return for that attention. What can be done to earn this "Return on Attention" or ROA? Through an ebusiness effort, the successful company will allow customers to get information about products or services quickly as well as allow them to customize the selection of that information or the configuration of products or services to be purchased.

Companies, at their essence, are really learning organizations. According to consultants Larry Downes and Chunka Mui, companies will reinvent themselves[10], learning from the information they gain about their environment. If you're reading this book because information retrieval and/or analysis is your profession, then you can thank this concept for your job. The successful company will enable the learning available from the immediate feedback and observe which aspects of its products or services customers are requesting most. They will track what those customers are doing in the self-service areas. They will use all of this as market feedback regarding the desirability of their offering. From what they have learned, they will analyze the information and determine what the customer will want next and be there with that offering, quickly, in time, before the competition. Perhaps before you.

This type of action will save the customer time for the attention that they paid. Realizing that they got a ROA, the customer will return to that successful company, the one which manages the curse so sweetly, again and again. What this successful company has found, in other words, is a way to give the customers back time while dealing with the curse. They've, at least partially, fulfilled the promise made back in the early 1980s. Time is a precious gift that the customers cannot buy for themselves. But if those successful companies can buy it for their customers, they will have those customers forever.

Oh. There is one other idea about time that I should mention before we move on. You probably all know about this already, especially if you have a teenager or a spouse who stays up until all hours of the night surfing the Web or kibitzing in chat rooms. The term "all hours of the night" should be the giveaway here. Yes. The Internet is a 24 hour environment. You've seen that term 24/7, 24x7, or 24x7x365 all over the place, haven't you? I know I have and I'm sick of it. I know the Internet is always on. I know that people can do their Internet business at any time of day.

People are staying up all over the world because they are simply over-stimulated by too many things going. They can't sleep because they won't sleep, afraid that they will miss something. A National Sleep Foundation poll said that 43 percent of adults admit to staying up too late because they are watching a screen, television or computer.[11]

Everyone who lives with anyone else should be well aware of this situation by now. But let's apply this concept to competitive analysis. Someone, who is open all the time, is a truly tough competitor because they are catering to those potential customers who don't want to miss anything.

*   *   *

Social, not Technical, Science

So, we've established that the New Economy is connected. And that these connections can, if managed properly, reduce costs. Because the costs, or the inputs, decrease, what happens by comparison is that the outputs increase. Efficiencies grow. And that growth becomes exponential, meaning that instead of a linear equation where one begets one, we have a situation where one begets two and then four and then eight and so on. Why does this happen in the New Economy? Well, it happens because the connected economy, as we have seen, is based on the movement of information. Information is a non-consumable good. It can be used by more than one party simultaneously.[12] Because of this characteristic, the cost to deliver decreases, exponentially, as more and more people use it and pass it along. As the costs decrease exponentially, the returns increase exponentially.

Network economy growth, being exponential, is similar to the growth of organisms. Like people. One begets two, then two beget four, and then four beget eight. You get the idea. The fuel for this New Economy growth is not the tweaking of the system to produce small improvements in efficiency as would be done in the industrial economy with its relatively linear, non-exponential functions. The key to exponential growth in the network economy is knowing about people. What makes them tick. How to make their lives easier. How to save people time. How to save people money. If people have more resources, they will use them, as Kelly says, for more exponential growth, furthering the network.[13] How does this affect business? Come on, you should be catching on by now!

If the key to exponential growth in the New Economy is knowing about people, then to run a business in the New Economy managers must seek out people who know about people. They must look for employees with a background or education in sociology, psychology, or anthropology.

Yes. You read that correctly. Anthropology.

You say, "Why? Those were the people in college without shoes, buzzed out, muttering to themselves. What could THEY know about business."

> *Anthropology—The science that deals*
> *with the social customs and*
> *cultural development of mankind*

"They" (the sociological other, yet again) know more about business than you think they do. And, surprisingly, they probably know more about business than they think they do.

Let's look at this people selection problem this way. When you took economics for the first time, did you think it was weird? Instructors not withstanding, economics itself really isn't weird. The problem you had was that you were thinking of economics as a quantitative subject. It really isn't. Yes, we do use a lot of math in economics; derivatives, integrals, exponents, and logarithms. But the basis of economics itself, what makes economics tick, is that it is essentially a SOCIAL science, not a mathematical science. If you went to a college without a business school, please remember that the economics course selections were in the social sciences part of the catalog, not the mathematics part of the catalog.

Economics is a social science because the answers to economics questions are based in social responses, the way in which we relate to our environment and the people around us. Remember back. Don't you recall all that talk about "rational man?" Or were you trying to figure out first derivatives at that time? Economic theory and the rules derived therefrom are based on the rational behavioral performance of people. Of course, sometimes, in the short run, people don't behave rationally. But in the long run, most do and it is from these behaviors that economic theory gains the strength to look at itself in the mirror every morning.

Anthropology (remember Mc Luhan?) is the study of how people relate to their culture. Anthropology can tell you why we relate to the things in the ways that we do. Services, products, people, systems, networks. All of these, and especially the Web, are part of our culture, big time. So, if you agree that economics is the basis of business and if you can see that economics is actually a social science, then you will understand how anthropologists can help run a business in the New Economy, where people drive the exponential growth through the employment of ideas about solutions communicated through non-consumable information.

*   *   *

Economic Webs

As stated in the previous section, networks will amplify growth. They are capable of taking the smallest hint of growth and multiplying it beyond all recognition. Not just electronic networks are capable of this, but any kind of network can do this. The nice thing about a network is that the growth it creates is, as mentioned previously, "organic." It spreads like an organism, exponentially. Not linearly, like a non-networked system. Ever hear of the "grapevine?" Whether the subject is a job opening, who's sleeping with whom, or who's sucking up to the boss, once a message is on the grapevine that message's recipients multiply. Once begets two, two beget four, blah, blah, blah. The grapevine is a network and its messages grow exponentially.

We talked earlier about how connections in an economy can reduce costs and how with lower inputs we get, by comparison at least, higher outputs. To put this in technical economic terms, it's an uncommon phenomenon known as "increasing returns," a concept originally explored by an economist named Brian Arthur. Increasing returns, or what we get out of networked growth, are the opposite of those diminishing returns that we learned about in economics class. With diminishing returns, output decreases as input increases. With increasing returns, it is, of course, the opposite. As output increases, input decreases. What a sweet little situation for business people!

Business people may interpret a situation with increasing returns as having unitary costs that continuously decrease, if they're lucky to the point of zero. They may hope those costs will reach zero, but they actually never will. Increasing returns inputs are asymptotic. Remember asymptotes? Those funny little curved functions in math class that you could never get to cross an X, Y, or Z axis, i.e., zero?

> *Asymptote—A mathematical curve approaching zero, but never reaching it.*

Costs for exponential growth experienced via a network will never be zero. But those costs will be considerably less compared to the linear output experienced in a non-networked system.

In a networked environment with increasing returns, we see the term "economic web,"[14] i.e. a network where the exponential output is created and enjoyed by the participants and their mutual dependency. That mutual dependency can be as complex as the supply of a product or service which is used complementarily by another in the economic web or the mutual dependency can be a simple as the members depending on each other to transmit messages within the economic web. As Kelly suggested, all business people participating in an economic web should realize that the increasing gains from the economic web might be reaped unequally by organizational or individual efforts in the web.[15]

So, what does that mean? Let me give you a simple example.

There is a grapevine where you work. There is a job opening for which you are perfectly qualified. The boss mentions to someone that he/she is searching for someone with X qualifications. That someone mentions this to two other someones. Those two other someones mention this to two other someones each. And so on until the message reaches you. You're perfectly qualified. You apply for the job and get it. Obviously you benefited the most. But how did others in the network benefit? They benefited by knowing that there was another job opening, thinking that they might be qualified, thinking that they might be able to earn more money, thinking that they were going to improve their lot in life and get out of the stinking job that they currently hold. The benefits to others in this case were psychological and fleeting, but they did exist, no matter how ephemeral. Remember. Every participant in an economic web benefits, but some benefit more. It's a little like George Orwell's Animal Farm. I'll leave you to make the connection.

Before participating in an economic web, a company, a competitor, should realize that many of the participants and not just one of them, per

Kelly, create the benefits of participating in an economic web.[16] Before entering into an economic web, management should ask this:

> *"Uh, excuse me. Will the growth in this network be created*
> *by network effects or through the efforts of*
> *any one company or person?"*

If the answer is the latter, run away screaming the following phrase, "I can't get away fast enough!" Companies should only move to be part of an economic web if the answer is the former. If the "web" depends on one company or person, then Hello?, it's not a web. It's a line, a non-networked system. And the growth will not be exponential and it will not be shared in any proportion.

From all of this we should understand the following. Your competitors, if they are smart and if they understand the foregoing, will be looking for a web with many different parts and participants so as to maximize network effects, so as to hop on some of those exponential returns. Some of those parts and participants may be complementary or some of those parts may be competitive. The value of complementary elements in a web is obvious, but the existence of competitive elements is not as apparent. Competitive elements in a web do not necessarily indicate danger. Often they will indicate quite the opposite.

Let's say we're looking at an economic web that sells things. As more potential customers look into this web, they will see many competitive offerings. The very presence of so many competitive elements will, by itself, attract qualified potential buyers. These buyers will evaluate the offerings. The buyers will flock to the superior offering, leaving the inferior offering to wither on the vine ("the increasing gains from the economic web might be reaped unequally by organizational or individual efforts in the web").

Those companies not gaining a share of customers, i.e. sales, will still benefit from network feedback, receiving information as to why their offering was not chosen. This information is invaluable to setting their offering on the right course, and it is available at little direct cost when created and managed within an economic web with increasing returns.

*   *   *

Increasing Demand

OK. You should be getting this by now. Time for a test.

> Question: *How much would you pay for the only fax machine in the world?*

Alright, calm down. There's no time limit. There's no proctor watching you. Let's just think about this one before answering.

Remember from economics class that as supply goes down, if demand remains stable, the price of something goes up. Low supply, high demand, high price. Right? EL WRONGO!

A fax machine is one of those things that derives its value from being networked.[17] If there was only one fax machine, it would be worth exactly zero, zed, zippo, goose eggs, zilch, nada, rien, nothing. Only when it is part of a network does it become valuable.

If you will, please remember basic economics class, the demand curve, or the price consumers will pay for various quantities of a good or service, slopes downward and to the right. This means that as the price for a product decreases, the quantity of a product demanded increases. There are a number of reasons for this effect, the foremost of which is diminishing returns. In this traditional theory there is a corollary that says the more we have of something the less we value it. This is one type of social, psychological, anthropological response.

But in the new, or networked, economy, the demand curve is turned around. The demand curve slopes upward. This means that as the price for the product increases, the quantity demanded of that product will also increase.

Do you need an aspirin yet?

Well, maybe you don't really need the aspirin. If we really want to get technical, the demand curve actually doesn't slope upward. What really happens is that with the supply curve of highly demanded goods relatively stable the demand curve shifts to the right, many times, in rapid succession. The effect of this movement is that it causes a series of equilibrium points, prices, which if connected by a line assume an upward sloping posture, an upward sloping curve. Populist economists in the New Economy have dubbed this as an upward sloping demand curve. I think that they know it is not actually a demand curve, but by calling it such they can get their 15 minutes of fame. Though in some ways by calling it an upward sloping demand curve, the concept is easier to grasp. But in other ways calling the demand curve shift an upward sloping curve just causes headaches.

Question: *So, either way you like it, upward demand curve or a series of demand curve shifts, what's behind this phenomenon?*
Answer: Network effects.

Network effects were examined in the previous section, the essence of which was "increasing returns." When applying network effects and increasing returns scenarios to a demand curve the result is that, per Kelly, as more of the products become available, those products become increasingly valuable because their value is based in network usage.[18] The products make increasing returns possible, so the price of those products should also increase. This is another type of social, psychological, anthropological response, one that takes place in a networked economy, only. Why then don't fax machines cost $1,000 a piece? Because even though that demand curve continues to shift to the right, exhibiting an increasing price for the product, the price increase is mitigated by manufacturing economies of scale, bringing down the cost of each successive machine produced, and, along with that reduction, the price. Ironic, isn't it? Ironic that Old Economy linear, manufacturing economies of scale should mitigate the price increases of products whose value rises due to their ability to be networked and provide increasing returns.

So what does all of this mean? It means that for a company, a competitor, to be successful, they should leverage the principle of increasing returns by offering an offering that is based on network effects.

*   *   *

Friction Elimination

Alright. I think you're getting this now. Let's have another test, just to be sure.

Question: *What's the meaning of electronic business?*

Most people don't even come close to the correct answer, or at least to what I believe is the correct answer.

Answer: *Serving customers is the most important meaning of business. Customer need fulfillment and serving customers at reduced cost are therefore the meanings of ebusiness.*

Without customers, no one eats.

Ask yourself that question again and honestly think about what your response is. Your response will indicate whether or not you truly believe that the Internet and other electronic business avenues can be used to make customers' lives easier. If you do proactively make their lives easier, that will in turn benefit your business. Just concentrate on the customer and the rest will follow. This is a prime principle of the Old Economy. And it won't change in the New Economy.

Today, what is at the heart of serving customers correctly, so as to satisfy them, and keeping costs low, so that a decent profit is created, is the technology that enables ebusiness. Search technologies will have the biggest and most profound impact affecting the way customer needs are met and profits are maximized in this New Economy.

Without information about goods and services, the consumer experiences something which economists call "information asymmetry" and which was explored by consultants John Hagel III & Marc Singer.[19] Some people also call this "friction." Call it what you will, what it means is that if all customers cannot get complete information on all the goods and services available to solve a particular customer problem, then that customer must make a purchase decision with incomplete information. Presently, this is almost always the case. Product information is then asymmetrical, meaning that not all persons have equal access to the information that will allow them to make a completely informed purchase decision. What results is a situation where the customer probably does not get the best product or service to apply toward the resolution of his/her problem.

Thus, a society gets people who are suboptimizing their solutions, through little fault of their own. The society does not, then, function at its peak, generating friction and inefficiency all the way.

Colloquially put, the above paragraph means that we can't always get all the info we need before we buy something, so we wind up settling for something that isn't exactly what we want because we couldn't find anything better and in the end it doesn't exactly solve our problem, anyhow and we're sorry we bothered at all.

New search technologies will help us reduce this information asymmetry, friction, and their resulting inefficiencies. One such technology being developed, at this writing, is XML language, or Extensible Markup Language. This is a variant of hypertext markup language (HTML) which is the standard language now used for Web sites. XML, and other future languages, will allow more exacting searches of ecommerce sites, allowing improved comparative searches to be made of product prices and features. These future languages will therefore allow persons to search the Internet more accurately for the products and services they desire.

Another technology being discussed, put forth in *Net Worth* by consultants Hagel & Singer, is that of the infomediary, sometimes referred to as a metamediary.[20] These entities will be companies holding customer profiles on preferences, likes, and dislikes. As third party companies, they will filter offers from sellers and seek out products and services for their buyer clients based on the parameters listed in those clients' preference profiles. The infomediary is also seen as performing many other functions to reduce asymmetry, and friction, making for a more efficient economic environment.

*   *   *

Brands Moribund

Thus, because of improved search technologies and infomediaries, with the reduction of friction one of the big changes in the New Economy will be the amount of power that buyers will have. One of the advantages that sellers had until now was that information asymmetry enabled them to hide some of the imperfections that were present in their products or services. This was sometimes good news for sellers. However, the information asymmetry would also hide some of the benefits of a seller's products and services.

Another problem that sellers had, and still do, is gaining the attention of potential buyers. That problem only increased through the 20th century because as sellers gained more and better technology with which to send marketing messages buyers were assailed with more and more of them. In an industrial age attempt to overcome the problems of: 1) information asymmetry hiding product and service benefits; and, 2) inattention, sellers established "brands."

The brand was intended to be a short, iconoclastic communication that would remain within the control of the seller. The brand was intended to communicate to buyers the product or service benefits and do it in a very short time period. They were going for maximum ROA. Buyers, not having access to perfect information (friction, remember?) nor having unlimited time, but wanting both, would attend to the iconoclastic brand messages and base their decision on the trust factor which became increasingly intertwined with the brand message as it was communicated over long time periods. Thus, the brand's creation was based upon information's asymmetry. But what will happen as information asymmetry is decreased by electronic business?

The importance of brands as business tools will decrease as well. Why? Because one of the functions of a brand is to communicate benefits quickly. If we have infomediaries searching for product benefits according to a customer profile, why, as Hagel & Singer put it, do we need to rely on a biased brand image controlled by the seller?[21] What this also means is that if sellers are basing their strategy on selling a quality product or service, then that offering will truly have to be of high quality. Or if the seller relies on a strategy of selling a low-cost product, that price must truly be low. Search technologies will quickly reveal inferior product features or prices that are not competitive. There will be no more hiding behind a brand in the New Economy.

*   *   *

Fractal Freedom

Hang on. We're almost finished with concepts. You've learned a lot. And because of it, you are ready to handle this section, the radical section.

Look at a tree, a plant, a cow, a person. They are all examples of fractals. Fractals, as observed by Davis & Meyer, are naturally occurring.[22] What are fractals? Fractals are systems where the principles and the nature of the system are the same at every level of that system.[23] An easy way to understand this is by looking at a person, an organism. The system starts at the main trunk, the torso. It branches out into legs and arms, which then branch out into toes and fingers. In other words, the torso grows cylindrical elements, like itself, followed by yet smaller cylindrical elements. If toes and fingers were to continue to grow, being fractal systems they would probably each sprout numerous smaller cylindrical elements. Please note, also, that this growth is exponential.

Now an organism is a system. Networks that facilitate adjustment to the environment around them connect systems. An economy is a system. If we apply a fractal view to the economic system, we can see that each level of the economy adjusts to influences in the same way, i.e., through the basic interaction of the supply and demand curves. But the company doesn't act as a fractal element of the larger system because, as suggested by Davis & Meyer, company departments run on predefined, politically motivated budgets, not the actual interaction of the supply and demand curves at the departmental level.[24]

> *Political Budget—A financial plan constructed to support goals not of the greater good.*

Therefore, companies short-circuit the fractal, and self-sustaining nature of the larger system in which they operate. Why do they do this? Political control of information and other resources by management. You know what I'm talkin' 'bout, Willis.

Supply and demand interactions operate on information, the more perfect the information, the more efficient the supply and demand dynamics. But if management controls the flow of information within the company in a "non-fractal" fashion, how can the company expect to function as efficiently, and as fractally, as the larger economic system of which it is a part? It is then at odds with a system that is supposed to ensure its survival.

As the New Economy heats up, with its promise of reduced information asymmetry, the market for real goods and services will function with more perfect information, increasing supply and demand interaction efficiencies.

In order to function more efficiently, or perhaps even to survive, companies must be willing to adopt internally the nature of the larger economic system in which they operate. This means the free flow of information within the company. P&L statements, balance sheets, customer profiles, production schedules, sales forecasts, the whole Magilla.

But what about security and competitive interests you say? There are ways to ensure the integrity of the information so it cannot be used against the company, but that is a subject for another book. What is important right here is to realize that companies must be restructured in the New Economy so as to serve as natural fractal extensions. They must also serve as organisms that may grow exponentially based on the free flow of information about and within the company and about the larger economic system in which the company operates.

Company, competitor, networks can facilitate this free flow of information. In this way, employees will be empowered to act in the best interest of the company, which in turn is in the best interest of themselves. It's a cycle, one that shouldn't be short-circuited.

*　　　　　*　　　　　*

Demon Demographics

Webster defines this as **the characteristics of human populations such as size, growth, distribution, and vital statistics.** In those vital statistics is the most vital of statistics, age.

I once saw an instructional movie entitled, "Who You Are is Where You Were When." How true. Our experiences at certain times of our lives defined our character, our philosophy, and our behavior. In short, our experiences shape the way we look at the world and relate to our culture and other cultures. Look. Anthropology appears on the scene again.

The experiences we had were largely shaped by the times in which we lived. The following discussion pertains only to the American society. The generation coming of age during the Great Depression and World War 2 tended to adopt conservative behaviors, necessitated by their financial and social circumstances. They banded together against a common foe, again necessitated by circumstances.

Their children, the Baby Boom, came of age in a time of social change and economic prosperity, creating behaviors with a more individualistic orientation. (Remember the "Me" Generation?) And their children, Generation X, are coming of age now at the birth of the information age, in a technological revolution, available to many rather than few. The tail end of the Boomers is riding this technological wave along with their children, but it is the Xers who are on the crest.

Because the Xers are on the leading edge at an impressionable time of their lives, their technological absorption rate is high and that will help change the landscape of commerce to one of ecommerce. Three things are needed to change the American commercial environment.

Right now, at the time of this writing, the leading edge of Boomers is in their early fifties. Their oldest Gen X children are in their mid-twenties, only having recently joined the workforce, embarking on careers. The Xers have the affinity for the technology. Do you know of a 25 year-old that does not understand Web-speak? To change the American commercial landscape, the first thing that is needed is an understanding of, and a comfort level with, Internet technology. The second thing that is needed is money.

Moolah to spend at ecommerce sites. At the start of their working lives, discretionary income is not large, but it will grow.

Moolah—American slang for money

As the Xers gain work experience, in about five to ten years, they will begin to enter their prime earning period. Simultaneously, they will begin to give birth, move up the career ladder, and just generally have less time in their lives. That brings us to the third thing needed and that is a lack of time. And as the Xers mature they will experience that.

So in about 5 to 10 years from the publication date of this book, it is expected that ecommerce will become a dominant force in business. Why? Because by that time, the Xers will be ready, willing, and able, the three economic conditions behind a purchase.

The Xers will be ready with an understanding of how to use Internet technology to their advantage. They already know how.

The Xers will be willing to make extra time for themselves by saving it through the use of efficient services like infomediaries.

And they will be able to do this because their incomes will be steadily increasing.

It's all in the cards. It's all in the demographics. We're already past the point of no return.

*   *   *

Managerial Flux

OK. Hang on. We're almost finished with the concepts section of this book. This is the last one. Anytime something new in business comes along there are different ways to look at it. There are always plenty of books written by too many gurus saying far too much. Some of the things said in those books vary from guru to guru while others are just a rehash of what has been said before. When the New Economy hit town, those gurus foamed at the mouth. They went into overdrive. 'Here is something really new,' they thought. 'Something that we can churn out about four or five books apiece on.'

Well, although I wax sarcastic, the New Economy really is a new type of idea, one that comes along far too infrequently, like the invention of movable type. Running a business in the New Economy is something new. One of the more outstanding things that makes it new is that there are proportionately fewer people to do the same jobs than there would be in a physical world company. The reason for this is, as we have alluded, the substitution of technology in the place of labor.

Now, one of the things that I think is really cool about a New Economy company is that you can do so much more with so much less. What I mean here is that because you're asking a bunch of computers to do things that people did before, you can reduce the possibility of mistake, making a better company with fewer people. This, of course, could have a downside, but let's just think about the upside for now. One of the upside factors is that because you have fewer folks in the organization, the folks that remain are, by definition at least, closer to the customer, closer to the source of funds used to operate the company, closer to the breadbasket, closer to the meal ticket.

Downes & Mui discussed the significance of this shrinking of the organization as one of getting the remaining employees to achieve customer intimacy through the technology.[25] With this new found economic intimacy goes a responsibility, though. The employee must serve the customer as they would serve themselves. Sort of a golden rule of customer service. Since there are fewer employees, they are more "visible" to the customer and therefore must be less prone to mistakes. I believe one of the best ways to prevent employees from making mistakes is to give them the information that they need to do their jobs. We touched on this idea in the Brands Moribund section. Now let's look at it from a management perspective.

Giving employees full access to company information means that much present management must change. Normally management is all-uptight about doling out information. They like to let employees know very little about the operation. They're usually very stingy with the info. But to survive in this New Economy, managers must change their mindset. The traditional means of doing business can no longer always be applied.[26] Flux is here to stay, and management must be aware that the occurrence of flux will be constant.[27]

THE ISSUES

We've examined some basic concepts important to understanding the difference between online business and offline business. As previously stated, if as a competitive intelligence analyst you have no knowledge of these concepts, it will be difficult, if not impossible, for you to recognize what is special about ebusiness. As a consequence, you will not be able to identify the strengths, or weaknesses, of an ecompetitor. Along with your existing competitive intelligence research tool set, the conceptual background will act as a foundation upon which you may build solid ebusiness competitive analysis skills.

The remainder of *Dangerous Competition* poses specific questions, based on the concepts, that the analyst should pose in order to properly assess an ecompetitor. The Issues are divided into five sections:

- Site Content & Functionality

- Strategy & Mission

- Marketing

- Management & Organization

- Financial

Let's start with some basic things first, then we'll work our way up to the more complex issues.

Site Content & Functionality

Quite frankly, what we'll discuss in this first Issues section I find to be somewhat boring, because it is basic. But just because it is basic and boring, doesn't mean that it isn't important. How many basic and boring things do you do in your life that are still important? How about the laundry?

"Every hero becomes a bore at last."—*Emerson*

Well, I can't make doing laundry more exciting for you, but I will try to make this section as exciting as possible. If you find that I have failed, please look forward to the rest of the book because the balance is not as pedestrian as this section.

What should be assessed on a competitive site?

Doing an assessment of a competitor's Web site content and functionality is usually what most people call ebusiness competitive intelligence. This would be analogous to the fact that many people believe getting some news articles on an offline competitor is what Old Economy competitive intelligence is all about. Oh, those poor misguided souls. But you, as a competitive intelligence professional, should instinctively know that just getting some articles about a competitor would produce an inadequate assessment. Certainly getting some articles about the competition is a good place to *start*, and so is an assessment of your ebusiness competitor's Web site. When checking out a competitor in the ebusiness space, visit their Web site. While visiting, be aware that there are nine things that should be done when checking a competitive Web site.

1. Navigate Pages.
2. Time Loadings.
3. Send Email.
4. Look for Contact.

5. Check Consistency.

6. Search For and In The Site.

7. Identify eCommerce.

8. Find Policies.

9. Find Community.

1. **Navigate Pages**. Experience how easy it is to move from page to page. The analyst should look for broken links, meaning links that are dead, which don't do anything when clicked. Dead end links should also be identified. Dead ends are when a link takes one to a page where other links to the site, or other external sites, are unavailable. This situation necessitates the Back button being employed and is usually considered bad manners in Web design.

2. **Time Loadings**. When navigating the pages, the analyst should time how long it takes for pages to load on different speed modems. Examples of different speed modems, from slowest to fastest, would be dial-up or wide band such as DSL, cable, or T1.

> *DSL—Digital subscriber line.*
> *A local telephone company service*
> *which allows high speed Internet service*
> *over ordinary copper phone lines.*

If the analyst does not have access to different speed modems, there are Web sites available which will determine page loading speeds for different modems. We'll discuss this issue in more detail later in the book.

3. **Send Email**. Send product/service questions via email to customer service and see how long it takes them to respond, or if they respond at all. Ask them ridiculously simple questions as well as more difficult questions so that you may assess response time on each type. What you are testing by checking load time or ease of navigation or the answering of email is the competitor's sensitivity to the savings of time for their site

visitors and/or customers. By putting up a Web site the ecompetitor is telling its customers, at least indirectly, that they wish to save customers some time, that precious resource. But if the pages are not intuitively navigable, or if the pages take an abnormally long time to load, or if the customer service reps don't email back, then the ecompetitor is just generating frustration, and in the end possibly costing the customer more time than it is trying to save them.

4. **Look for Contact**. Try to locate the company's contact information. Easy to find? Make a note. All too often, ebusiness companies hide their contact information two or three screens deep, if it is on the site at all. I've never been able to figure out exactly why companies sometimes make contact so difficult. It is either because they don't want you to contact them (fly-by-night operation or they want to make it hard for process servers to find them) or they just plain forget to put the information there. You say, "That's ridiculous. How could they be stupid enough to forget their contact information?" Hey, Chuck. That's nothing. I've seen companies who have forgotten to put their phone numbers in print advertisements and television commercials. How could they be stupid enough for that? It happens. People are people. If they don't put the contact information on a site location easy to access, then whether intentional or accidental it's just another example of how they are not saving the visitor's time.

5. **Check Consistency**. As a competitive intelligence analyst looking at an ecompetitor, you should check the consistency of information from one page to the next. Look for completeness and clarity of product or service information. Check to see if the benefit of the product or service is clearly communicated. Have others read these pages to see if it is clear to them just what the competitor brings to the table. Far too often in Webland, the explanation of what the company or its product or services do is elusive, especially with technology companies.

6. **Search For and In The Site**. Search for the competitive site on search engines and directories like Excite, Alta Vista, and Yahoo. Note their rankings in the search results. Check back on the competitor's site to see if they

are using techniques to optimize the search results such as popular key-words and descriptions or special coding such as extensible markup lan-guage, XML. Compare the search results with those of other competitors. Look to see if your competitor's products and services communicate supe-riority in the quality and price relationship over others. This level of supe-riority will be important to the ecompetitor as Internet search technology improves, because new search technology will quickly uncover any entry that is not absolutely superior.

The analyst should also check the site to see if it is internally searchable. Such a facility eases navigation for visitors and saves them time.

7. **Identify eCommerce.** Is the site fully ecommerce enabled? That is to say, can a person actually make a purchase using only the site and not any other medium of communication? That's what ecommerce means, at least in this book. If the site is a B2C site (business to consumer), the analyst should make several purchases over a series of days or weeks. Track and identify how long it takes for the product to be delivered. If the site offers alternative methods of shipping, try different methods to see if they have any effect on how quickly the merchandise arrives. Also, try purchases at different times of the year, such as Christmas and Hanukkah, Mother's Day, and at the end of fiscal quarters.

Is the site ecommerce enabled, but B2B (business to business)? If so and the product or service can legitimately be used by your company, make that purchase and do all the things we talked about above for the B2C site.

The point here is that what you're doing is simply playing customer. Once you act legitimately as a customer, you will easily be able to assess whether or not you liked the experience you had with the ebusiness ven-dor. That they happen to be your competitor is an added benefit to the opinion that you will form.

8. **Find Policies.** The competitive intelligence analyst should also search the site for return policies and procedures. Are those policies easy to find? Or are they buried several pages deep, along with that contact info? It

shouldn't be, but that's often the case. After the merchandise arrives, follow the instructions to return the merchandise. Track how long it takes to get a refund or credit. Assess the overall ease of product return. Again, here the time saving concept is at issue.

9. **Find Community**. Look also to determine if the site offers community and personalization. Community would include things like allowing customers to contact and communicate with other customers. Topics of these communications may be the resolution of mutual problems using the ecompetitor's offering. If this is the case, the competitive intelligence analyst should investigate to determine if the ecompetitor monitors and/or moderates the communications. It should be obvious why this would be important. Personalization includes things like allowing customers to customize their network interface, such as their Web page content. Many customers like to include personalized information about their company, or stock quotes, or the weather, or pictures of their children on ecommerce pages visited regularly.

∗ ∗ ∗

Strategy & Mission

Has your competitor chosen an ebusiness mission?

This might seem like a ridiculous question, but just because someone is on the Internet doesn't necessarily mean that they've thought that whole move through. In all likelihood, one of the things that they haven't thought through is mission.

Let's first decide what an ebusiness mission is.

Far too often I have heard stressed and harried clients say, "We've got to get on the Internet." My eyebrows jump. My heartbeat quickens. My attention is piqued. My considered and erudite response to that statement is "Why?" They then look at me as if I have two heads saying: "You're the competitive analysis guy! We should be there because our competition is there." 'Hoo, man,' I think. 'What a well-thought out answer, you reactionary you.'

Are we suddenly like lemmings? Oops. What do I mean "suddenly?" Businesses have been following their competitors' moves for centuries without truly understanding or even considering the impact those moves will have on their business or even on the competitors' businesses. So here we are. Smack dab in the New Economy with all of its changes and new demands. At least we can relax in the knowledge that one element of business management has not as yet changed. People still follow the crowd and sometimes do dumb things for even dumber reasons.

But no matter. The mission of this book, the specific task to be performed, is not to attempt to change human behavior. That's been tried ad infinitum, even ad nauseum. The mission of this book is to help you in the analysis of your ebusiness competitors, to help you understand their behavior, to help you understand if they have really thought everything out, or if they are just following the crowd. If they are doing the latter, then they're not so dangerous. But if they have accomplished the former, then look out. To examine the competitor's ebusiness mission, we will look at the following six items. And when in those items I say "it," I mean the performance of ebusiness.

1. Who does it.

2. Why they do it.

3. How they do it.

4. What they do.

5. When they do it.

6. Where they do it.

1. **Who does it**. Let's talk about the "who" first. This should be on the top of your to-do list because there are ebusiness competitors coming out

of the woodwork that you have never heard of before and after next Tuesday you may indeed never hear from again. That's the way it is in ebusiness. The competitive intelligence analyst will need to identify not only its traditional competitors as ebusiness examination targets, but will also need to smoke out some non-traditional competitors as well. Because of comparatively low barriers to entry in ebusiness, it is somewhat easy to encroach into new markets. This makes for a lot of competitors entering a potentially lucrative market. By polling customers, the competitive intelligence analyst will be able to identify quickly relevant ecompetitors inside and outside of the traditional competitive set.

2. **Why they do it**. Why does a company exist? Now, if you have to scratch your head before answering, maybe you should go back to the basics and start selling lemonade on the corner. You'll soon realize **that the mission of business, offline as well as online, is to satisfy needs and wants**. Forget that stuff they told you in business school about the goal of a business being to enrich its shareholders. That's a legal definition. Not a business one. Enrichment of shareholders is a secondary mission which will follow from the completion of the first mission. They should teach you this not only on the first day of business school, but on the first day of elementary school. They don't teach you this though and that complicates everyone's lives right from the jump, but that's the subject of another book.

> *The Jump—American slang for*
> *the start, the beginning.*
> *Often referred to as Jumpstreet.*

3. **How they do it**. The mission of an electronic business is no different from that of any other business, to satisfy needs and wants. But, what differentiates the ebusiness from a brick & mortar business is that the ebusiness may accomplish this basic mission in a different way.

The ebusiness uses electronic means to create the business processes it employs to fulfill the needs and wants. Web sites, CRM systems, databases, legacy system interfaces, blah, blah, and more blah. I'm not going to bore you with a laundry list of ebusiness tools. (There's that concept of laundry being boring again.) What is important here (highlight this sentence, please) is that the ebusiness employs a "how," i.e., tools, to bring about a "what" that differs from those of physical businesses.

4. **What they do**. The "what" is a company that relies less on physical assets to meet its customer needs and more on brainpower to ameliorate the problems of time ("when") and distance ("where") which plague all customers everywhere while doing it all at a lower cost than physical world counterparts.

5. **When they do it.**

6. **Where they do it.**

So, we have a "what," a company that offers its goods and/or services 24 x 7 ("when") to virtually any location on the planet ("where"). Prior to this configuration, 1994 and before, customers had to do business on the time schedule of the vendor and in a place the vendor could reach. These are two very limiting and finite dimensions over which customers exercise little control.

Thus, following from the foregoing, let's repose the question. Has your competitor chosen an ebusiness mission? The answer is "yes" if they meet your criteria of being a significant competitor and:

(1) employ an electronic business system, which through customer interface enables the customer to serve itself at any time and from anyplace on the planet, *and*

(2) that system makes the customer's life easier, less expensive, and saves the customer time, and meets customer needs and wants.

If the competitive ebusiness does not meet these mission prerequisites, then they probably didn't think out an actual ebusiness mission. They are probably just following the crowd.

Please note that the ebusiness system can use any type of an electronic network, the Internet, a telephone system, a private data network, or wireless Web networks. However, in this book when we refer to an ebusiness system, we will be referring to the Internet, and the Web in particular.

The saving of time is an important element in ebusiness because time is a finite resource. Once it is expended, we can never retrieve it nor can we make any more of it. So, if an ebusiness can save some of it upfront for its customers, those customers can feel all the richer and have a more positive attitude about the company who helped them "make" time. eBusinesses are uniquely positioned to achieve these "where" and "when" elements. If an ebusiness does not accomplish these goals, then they don't have a true ebusiness mission, and they are not truly an ebusiness, even though they have a Web site.

> *"Havin' a Web site doesn't make you an ebusiness."*
> *—Dieter Kruger*

eCompetitors maximizing time savings for their customers are providing that all important ROA, Return on Attention. The return is a resource that cannot be created, only saved.

Answering this question of the presence of an ebusiness mission is of paramount importance. If the ecompetitor is able to save its customers' time through their ebusiness system, the customer will be more likely to patronize your ecompetitor than your company. The impact upon your company for the delivery of a ROA is obvious.

The questions that follow through the end of the book may be categorized into one or more of the who, what, where, when, why, how topics of mission. They all fit. But I'd rather not tell you which questions fit into which topics. That would ruin some of the fun, as well as most of the learning exercise. You be the judge.

What key processes can support the competitive ebusiness mission?

In order for any company to complete its mission, it must first arrange its assets in such a way that they form processes that will achieve mission completion. Sounds logical. Processes important to the completion of an ebusiness mission must be organized in a way to produce a competitive advantage and complete the mission better than that ebusiness down the block. Important ebusiness processes, which are suggested from various sources[1], are:

- offer creation,
- order taking,
- logistics or service delivery, and
- customer service.

The answer to this question is important because although your ecompetitor may have as a stated goal the savings of time for its customers, if the ecompetitor does not have the requisite quality of process in place, reaching the goal will just be an elusive dream. As a competitive analyst, you must know the likelihood of the ecompetitor reaching mission completion. Assessment of these four processes will help you reach an opinion of that likelihood.

Offer Creation. The creation of the offer is an important process upon which the ebusiness competitor can bet its success. Per Davis & Meyer, the term "offer" is used rather than the terms product or service because there has been a merging of product and service so that the two are no longer as distinct as they once were in the physical world.[2] Their union in ebusiness has become known as "offer" or sometimes "offering." We'll discuss the concept in more detail later in this book.

Now, keep this in mind for the next time you open a lemonade stand. Successful offer creation depends upon the interpretation of customer needs and wants. The really formidable ebusiness competitors will obtain profile information about customers in an effort to define wants and needs so that offers may be created and extended to meet those wants and needs. The attainment of such profile information is not easy, but gathering and managing it is often simpler than the corresponding job in the offline world.

Even more formidable and fierce ecompetitors will analyze more extensively this information so that the ecompetitor is able to create an offer *prior* to the time that the customer even knows that it wants that particular offer. This type of anticipatory product development behavior is a critical process in ebusiness because it saves the customer search time.[3] How does it save the customer time you ask? It saves time because as soon as the customer starts to recognize the desire in the deepest and darkest corners of their Id, there is the offering, online, that will satisfy those arising desires. Such an approach represents the mark of an aggressive and dangerous ecompetitor. How would the competitive intelligence analyst recognize this capability?

Identifying the ecompetitor's ability to gather information from customers is straightforward. An examination of the competitive site will reveal this capability. The analysis of the competitor's ability to anticipate desired offers may be accomplished through the monitoring of the offers made on the site. Offers that appear to be "leading edge" or ones that may seemingly have no apparent market may be the ones developed from the anticipatory research.

Order Taking. The taking of the order is another important process to be analyzed in support of a competitive ebusiness mission. Of course, because of the term "order taker" being disparagingly applied to some types of salespeople, we may think that electronic order taking is a simple matter. Quite the contrary. The creation of an electronic order taking system is a technically complex matter of integrating legacy order and database systems on the back end with the Web or customer interface system on the front end.

Legacy System—A proprietary system in place in a company. The system is not linked to the outside world.

If you have ever been to an ecommerce trade show, you'll have seen about sixty zillion different products for interfacing legacy systems with Web front-ends.

The ecompetitor must possess or hire the proper technical talent in order to merge these systems properly. Often publicity will be made revealing whom or what is masterminding the integration tasks of various ecompetitors. As of this writing, from a competitive intelligence perspective many companies are not too smart in terms of the press releases they let out on their ebusiness efforts. They want the world to know that they are cutting the edge of the virtual and, from an intelligence control perspective, they get sloppy, blurting out information that can be used, to advantage, by competitive intelligence analysts.

Based on this flow of ebusiness related press releases, the analyst may make assessments as to the efficacy of any of the talent assembled for that task. Other than the order taking system's technical capability, the competitive intelligence analyst must also be alert to the non-technical elements. These elements would include such things as the amount of offer customization allowed, the ability of the customers' to check on and/or change orders in process, and the possibility for human interaction when desired by the customer, i.e., the availability of live customer service personnel online to assist with aesthetic selection issues or just to handhold in general. The availability of offer customization in this process is particularly important as it adds additional process value for the customer. Putting the "custom" back into customer is something which many businesses, offline as well as online, have forgotten. The advent of ebusiness systems allows companies to do this on a very cost-effective basis. I'll raise this custom idea again later.

A short digression is needed here. In this book, I refer to ebusiness as being that which is conducted via a Web site. However, as was hinted at previously, a broader definition of ebusiness is the conducting of commerce through any electronic means. These means include telephones, fax, and personal digital assistants, and/or wireless PDAs. Although this book is focused on the Web site approach to ebusiness, I do not take the position that other electronic avenues should be ignored. On the contrary, the customer should be allowed to place an order, and to service that order, through any electronic means that is desired by that customer. Thus, the competitive intelligence analyst should also be alert for competitive order taking methods which employ these other avenues. These other avenues should be available because some customers, even today, are just plain afraid of the Web, for a variety of reasons, and will refuse to place orders via the Web. For an ecompetitor to disregard the desire of some customers to place orders, even orders that originate on a Web site, through some other electronic means, is myopic and will cause that competitor to be much less dangerous.

Logistics and Service Delivery. Getting the product there or completing the service are also important to the completion of an ebusiness mission. The competitive analyst needs to look for how the rival product or service, i.e., offering, are delivered to the ultimate customer. If the offering can be digitized, such as information can, the analyst should observe if the ecompetitor allows for the offering to be delivered online, with all of the low-cost benefits that that implies. If the offering is in the analog world, i.e., everything other than digital, the analyst should discover if the ecompetitor has product or service delivery depots in key geographical locations, poised to serve the market segments it pursues. This type of analysis for the distribution of physical products or face-to-face service purveyance differs little from the type of competitive analysis performed on non-ebusiness companies.

Customer Service. And a fourth process to be analyzed is customer service, or what we refer to here as primarily after-sale service. As suggested earlier, the analyst should examine the ebusiness competitor to discover the level of effort necessary to return goods, secure refunds, and gain technical assistance or to complain about product or service. If the ecompetitor requires that all of this process be done in an analog fashion, then they are likely costing themselves a lot more money than is necessary.

"If you want to know what a man is really like, take notice how he acts when he loses money."—New England Proverb

Just as the ecompetitor should allow customers to order using whatever means they desire, the ecompetitor should also allow the customer to seek service by whatever means is desired by the customer. If that option is available, some will inevitably choose virtual customer service, which will decrease costs for the ecompetitor. This is not to say that the decrease of costs should be the ecompetitor's first goal. This is to say that the ecompetitor's goal should be rather to allow the customer to solve their problem through any means desired by the customer.

Additionally, the analyst should be alert for those competitor brick & mortar outlets strategically located within the market area. If the ebusiness competitor allows its products to be returned through the physical channel, then this procedure offers the customer yet another option in the customer service process. Such a competitive set up makes that ecompetitor very competitive and very dangerous.

Do they Zero Time?

Earlier we discussed how, in one of its critical processes used to complete an ebusiness mission, an ebusiness competitor will assemble an offer in such a way that the features of the offer anticipate those desired by the customer. By performing this feat of mindreading, the ecompetitor seemingly "responds" to a need or desire in virtually no time at all, i.e., it appears to take them no time to respond to the desires of its marketplace[4] and formulate an offering that meets the needs of the customer base. This prescient approach stupefies customers and baffles competitors. It is not mystical. Nor is it magical. It is called "Zero Time."[5]

Of course, it is not true that it takes the ebusiness competitor no time to research the customer, define its desires, and create and produce an offering that can satisfy those desires. Let's face it. They don't have magicians on the staff. What that ecompetitor does have, though, is an electronic business system configured so that it may identify incipient demand and then create the product or service that fills the demand once the demand is realized by customers. Seemingly, the offering appears out of nowhere, conjured by a genie in no time at all.

The issue of Zero Time is important for the competitive intelligence analyst to address because an ebusiness competitor with this capability has the ultimate speed to market and will gain first mover advantage in every market segment to which the Zero Time capability is effectively applied. But there must be a caveat here. That caveat is that Zero Time prevails as a competitive tactic only if the ecompetitor is able to extract meaningful and detailed information from its customers and prospective customers. There's a problem here, Bub.

The problem is that in these days of Internet privacy controversy and permission marketing, it is doubtful that many ecompetitors will be able to obtain much meaningful information with which to construct Zero Time. Look at it this way. Do you think thrice about leaving your personal information and thoughts on a Web site? Yet, through membership programs and privacy policies, a few ecompetitors will be able to extract meaningful information through permission-based programs. It is those ecompetitors who will be truly dangerous.

> *"If we don't succeed, we run the risk of failure."*
> —*Dan Quayle, Former U.S. Vice President*

Has the ecompetitor chosen a strategic direction, or is function following form?

This question relates to the "Is it cool?" site design philosophy that pervaded the Web back in the early days of 1994 through 1998. But in recent years, though, the gewgaws and doodads have been minimized on sites of businesses large and small. The terms "gewgaws" and "doodads" are very highly technical Web design terms representing techniques of Web site design often employed by Gen X site designers. Let us proceed from here agreeing that these techniques are a lot of crap that don't really do much to solve customers' problems or help to improve the profit potential of the site.

Once, in a client meeting, while going over the strategic approach of their site, one of the client's employees, a Gen Xer, said the following. "Yeah, and we should have like puzzles and trivia and other bitchin' stuff on the site to help make it sticky." I said, "Cool." Just trying to slip in with the lingo. "But how do these things solve our customers' problems?" He just gave me a blank stare saying, "Oh. I guess they don't."

That was in early 1999. Please excuse him. That guy was a holdover from the early days of the commercial Web, where site designers were loading up sites with a lot of stuff such as blinking words, puzzles, sound bites, flashing lights, spinning globes, trivia, dancing bears, and anything else for which they could cop a programming script and a link. This kind of nonsense got passed around from one site to the next until many sites started to look alike. Too much alike. The result was sites that looked "cool" but really didn't convey any type of business message, i.e., they did not solve their customers' problems. What was happening there was that the business function of these sites was taking second place to the form that was achieved by using gewgaws. Why did businesses allow this to happen? My answer is this.

Think about the days before 1994 when the word web was not capitalized and when it was just something between a duck's toes or in the corner of your cellar. Then, the children of the Baby Boomers were very young adults, 18 to 21, undefined and apathetic, unlike their parents whose generation, conceived in the rejoice of war ended, distinguished themselves at a similar age by fighting social injustice and extinguishing a senseless war whose goal seemed nothing more than the expenditure of their then young lives. Unlike their parents, the Boomer children chose no cause against which to rail, no politics to steel them, no revolution to lead, no wrongs to right. They were looked at by the popular press as bland, plain vanilla, blasé. They were called "Brand X." The name stuck and their generation came to bear that title.

Since they weren't out demonstrating against a war or trying to right a social wrong, after their homework was done they found themselves with a lot of time on their hands. The PC was becoming popular then and they learned its ins and outs and wherefores and whys. When the Internet hooked them up, their computer knowledge multiplied. Suddenly, they were at once a force and a focal point. They were the "experts" in something. And we anointed them as the leaders of this revolution. When the commercial Web exploded into the business scene, the Xers were ready and led the way.

In the early days about the only persons who knew how to do Web programming were the Generation Xers, people who, because of their young age, had little to no business management experience. But businesses wanted to get on the Web. They just *had* to get on the Web. They couldn't wait. We'll come back to this idea later. So, they had to put that task in the hands of the Xers who often jumped into the job with unbounded relish and enthusiasm and little or no supervision. Why no supervision? That's the fault of management, usually Boomers. Management had no idea of what was going on anyway, so supervision seemed to be superfluous. Management thought "Let's let those kids go crazy and it will define itself."

> *Supervision—In the early days,*
> *something businesses would*
> *have given Gen X Web designers*
> *if the businesses knew anything about*
> *the Internet*

Consequently and unfortunately, the design (form) was allowed to define the strategy (function) which the business would pursue online.

This type of irresponsible approach has subsided as the commercial Web has matured. At this writing in 2000, management is smartening up. Many sites are giving up the function following form approach and have now reversed the process to its proper sequence. The reason for this is twofold. First, businesses discovered that there wasn't enough bandwidth through which to jam all of those doodads. Narrowband, or those clunky dial-up modems that far too many of us use to connect to the Internet, kept too many people waiting too long and they tuned out too fast. Too bad. Management saw that they were not getting too much of a return out of this so that told the Xers not to put in too many geegaws. Second, upper management has awakened to the fact that they were letting a bunch of inexperienced kids effectively run the electronic side of the business, and that they weren't getting very good results. The reason for those results? Right. Function was following form. If function followed form in the offline world, far too many people would be on the unemployment line.

The way in which the competitive intelligence analyst can tell if function is following form is to examine an ecompetitor's Web site along two dimensions.

- A clear understanding of what the competitor is selling.
- A clear understanding of customer benefits purveyed by the product or service sold via the site.

If, as a competitive intelligence analyst, you can gain a clear sense along both of these dimensions, and if the site is not littered with a lot of gewgaws and doodads, then function is probably not following form.

Has the competitor supplanted value chain inefficiencies with technology?

Folks like to bandy about that term "value chain" here in the New Economy. Those are usually the folks who wear black turtleneck sweaters and, if male, a goatee. In case you don't have any black turtleneck sweaters in your drawer, let's just discuss briefly and simply what the heck a "value chain" is.

The value chain is the progression of steps needed to transfer value from a producer of goods or services to the consumer of those products, or vice versa. From the time commerce began, this chain has been decreasingly comprised of human labor. Human labor has been used decreasingly because humans are a problem, they must do things like eat everyday. So, they must be paid. Thus, the incorporation of people into a process makes that process expensive. There's another problem. People are, as we have all heard, imperfect. Put humans in a process and it becomes imperfect, slowing the system, further increasing costs.

When examining an ecompetitor, the analyst must look at the chain of elements employed by the ecompetitor to transfer its value, observing if any of those elements have been replaced by a technical interface. For instance, a manufacturer which retails directly has removed from the value chain the intermediaries of the wholesaler and retailer, each of which would place an extra percentage of margin on the final product, adding to the cost paid by the ultimate customer. Usually in ebusiness, the enabler behind the manufacturer eliminating the wholesale and retail steps of the value chain is the fact that the manufacturer no longer needs to rely upon the wholesaler and retailer to mitigate the problems of time and distance which separate the customer from the manufacturer's product. eBusiness systems achieve that mitigation at a cost much lower than that which humans can achieve alone. This is a relatively basic strategic concept in ebusiness, the pursuit of efficiency through the supplantation of labor for technology. The competitive intelligence analyst should always examine the ecompetitor to find if that ecompetitor has discovered the concept of space and time mitigation via technology, and if that concept is employed to the max.

What is not so basic a concept is not the study of which value chain element has been supplanted, but the study of how those elements resist the supplantation; and this is where it gets a little dicier for the competitive intelligence analyst. If the analyst is studying wholesalers and retailers as discrete competitors or as elements of a competitive value chain, then the analyst must not consider those elements as obsolete just because it is in ebusiness fashion and just because they can be supplanted in the value chain. Wholesalers and retailers in the age of ebusiness can and do discover a whole new life independent of their previous suppliers. It's not over until the fat lady sings.

The Fat Lady—American slang
referring to the end of
a program or show

Analysts should study those wholesaler and retailer competitors to identify that competitor's potential to bring things to its offering, other than the normal core services and product. An example of what to look for would be a wholesaler disintermediated by manufacturers going direct to customers via an ebusiness system, adding additional services to their wholesale offerings such as logistics analysis, logistics management, and credit analysis. Another example of what to look for is suggested by strategy consultant Michael De Kare-Silver as a retailer adding more "atmosphere" to its store, making the retail experience an aesthetic feast, e.g., special events, celebrity appearances, sights, sounds, food, something glamorous that cannot be accomplished online.[6] These things could be considered as the physical counterpart of the electronic gewgaws and doodads which I so specifically dismissed previously as not meeting customers' needs. Yet, they are not the same. The electronic store doodads clog bandwidth and discourage people from accessing a site. Physical store doodads do not prevent people from getting into the store, rather these things draw people in. Physical store doodads are also not the same as electronic doodads because they are not ends in and of themselves. The Gen X designers tended to put the doodads in first without linking them to a business objective. The physical store doodads are created by folks with experience at retail management, and are intended to help customers realize their needs and wants.

In this age of virtuality a wholesaler or retailer, in order to compete with the mitigation of space and time by ebusiness systems, must endeavor to make its physical status an asset rather than endure it as a liability. To them, matter must matter. Both the wholesaler and retailer approaches mentioned above are at least some of the ways to counter disintermediation strategies. They represent differentiation strategies and are constructed in a way to lure the customer with even more of an "offering" than could be experienced through purchasing via a Web site. For the competitive intelligence analyst to overlook these counter-strategies would be a mistake.

"Mistakes are always initial."—Pavese

These supplantation issues for competitive intelligence analysts are important to grasp because many intermediaries have been cut out of the value chain by ebusiness, but they don't intend to go quietly. These intermediaries are reformulating their strategies to add more than traditional value to their piece of the chain. The competitive analyst must keep up with these changes.

Does the competition leverage increasing returns from an economic web?

Highlight that question up there. This is one of the most important issues that can be addressed by the competitive intelligence analyst, whether or not their competition's ebusiness effort targets increasing returns. If you learn nothing else from this book, learn about increasing returns or be toast. Now, I could give you a long and drawn out explanation of increasing returns, steeped in economic theory, bristling with algebraic and differential calculus equations. But I won't. I'll keep it simple. To tackle this issue completely, let's discuss:

(1) Achievement of Increasing Returns

(2) "Informationalize ^{SM}"

(3) Information vs. Product Dependency

(4) "Semi-Analog ^{SM}"

(5) Economic Webs

1. **Achievement of Increasing Returns.**[7] Quite simply, increasing returns occur when a company's unitary costs for an offering continually decrease in relation to the amount of revenue obtained for that offering. The key word here is "continually" because many businesses do experience increasing returns for a brief time period, but sooner or later, mostly sooner, those increasing returns disappear. This dynamic relationship of continuous increasing returns allows the business to benefit from marginal costs, costs which continually approach zero. Increasing returns are opposite those about which we learned in economics class, diminishing returns, which are naturally occurring and, in the industrial world, are difficult if not impossible to avoid. Increasing returns, as stated above, often appear in many business situations, at least for a brief time. But continuous increasing returns, those which we are interested in identifying in ebusiness, are often created when employing an ebusiness system.

The achievement of this type of increasing returns means that a company is using resources that can be continually productive without incurring incremental costs. No doubt this is good. Take, for instance, Web servers. They help companies achieve increasing returns. These nifty little machines have the ability to serve information repeatedly, with little or no additional cost to each service. You certainly can't say that about people working at a lemonade stand. The information that a Web server dishes out is particularly well suited to helping achieve increasing returns. Why? Because information, unlike lemonade, is a non-consumable good; many people can use it simultaneously, unlike a physical product, which can only be used by one person at a time. You can't drink someone else's lemonade if it has already been consumed, even if you wanted to. Yuck! But, you can read a Web page that one thousand other people are reading at the same time.

2. **"Informationalize^{SM}"** The most important element in reaching the point of continuous increasing returns is the ability to "informationalize^{SM}" a product or service. Without this ability, continuous increasing returns are unlikely to happen. An ecompetitor that can informationalize, i.e., convert

much of if not all of its product or service benefit to an informational form, will be able to experience increasing returns, exponentially, virtually to the point where the market ceases to demand their product or service. But until that point occurs, the informationalized product or service can be one which creates increasing returns. These "virtual widgets," as were previously discussed in the Size Doesn't Matter section of this book, will make your ecompetitor truly dangerous.

3. **Information vs. Product Dependency**. Realizing the importance of informationalizing and how it contributes to continuous increasing returns, the competitive intelligence analyst should determine the degree to which its competitor's ebusiness effort is reliant upon the exchange of either information or physical product for value. To easily assess this, the analyst would rate these two positions on a scale. If an ecompetitor rates more highly toward the exchange of physical product without being able to informationalize, then they will exhibit a competitive weakness. The weakness is that they will not be able to fully exploit the potential of increasing returns at an exponential rate, one of the things that makes ebusiness sexy. This inability to exploit continuous increasing returns is , of course, because the exchange of physical product requires more cost in the distribution equation. Creating things like warehouses and logistical systems, buying or leasing things like trucks, and other productive equipment tends to increase costs because these are things that cannot be used simultaneously by more than one customer.

4. **"Semi-Analog** SM**."** Thus, if the competitive intelligence analyst has determined that it is physical product upon which the competitor depends, the analyst should look again at its competitor's ebusiness operation. Does that competitor simply use the ebusiness interface as a substitute salesperson and continue to sell physical product through the traditional physical distribution channel? This format is called "semi-analog SM." The semi-analog format makes for a less dangerous competitor in that it does not support continuous increasing returns nearly as well as the informationalized format. If the ecompetitor follows the semi-analog

model, they will decrease their costs somewhat. But their cost decreases, and subsequent returns, will not be nearly as large as those of the competitor who has been able to reduce their product or service to an informational form, delivered digitally, repeatedly, repeatedly, repeatedly, repeatedly, again and again, without concern for time, distance, or increased cost.

Now, the foregoing has been quite supportive of the ecompetitor delivery of an informationalized virtual widget and the attainment of continuous increasing returns. But that discussion should not be construed to mean that physical products cannot be sold competitively over the Web or via any other electronic forum. They can be. They have been. They are. They will be. So, if you are in the non-virtual widget industry, don't kick back and think your company immune from ebusiness competitors. Remember that what I have said is critical to an ecompetitor's ability to sell successfully via electronic means is that ecompetitor's ability to reduce its product to an informational form. It's not easy, but it can be done. Just look at the automobile industry. Did you ever think a car could be sold online? Today, selling cars via the Web is one of the Internet's hottest ecommerce markets. This subject will be discussed further later in this book.

5. **Economic Webs.**[8] The last factor to check in determining whether an ecompetitor is truly pursuing increasing returns is the ecompetitor's participation in an economic web. No, that's not a bunch of people studying for the next economics exam at a local college. An economic web is a formally or informally organized system of sellers, each of whose offering contributes more economic value to the offerings of other system participants than if those offerings were unavailable.

An example of an informal economic web to which many people can relate is that of a flea market. At a flea market, there are many different types of vendors selling a vast selection of merchandise. Some of that merchandise is complementary and adds value to other merchandise offered at the flea market. For example, one booth may sell lamps without shades while a booth several rows over may sell the shades. Vendors come together in economic webs, either consciously or unconsciously, for three reasons:

1) the venue is relatively inexpensive;

2) many people will attend to the web; and,

3) sellers know that complementary products will be available, increasing the odds of sale while in the web.

The odds for vendors of a sale being completed are also increased in an economic web even if the web contains competitive offerings. Increasing returns may be pursued in an economic web because the presence of complementary or competitive offerings attracts many buyers, decreasing the unitary cost of buyer attraction for each web member.

A department store is another example of an economic web, one that is more formal in nature. The nature of a department store is similar to that of a flea market, except that the department store merchandise mix is intentionally organized to induce complementary sales and there is only one vendor. In the department store format, costs are reduced because the vendor can advertise the mix and amortize the overhead cost across the entire selection. Increasing returns are thus pursued. But unless the economic web, or its participants, are able to informationalize, any increasing returns achieved may be short-lived and discontinuous.

A more New Economy type of economic web example is the well-known WinIntelPC economic web. This is, of course, the convergence of the Windows® operating system, the Intel® microprocessor, and the personal computer, which together are certainly worth more than if one part existed independent of the other two. What would you do with an Intel® chip if you didn't have a PC?[9]

Discussing economic web theory is very hip. You can be even hipper by wearing a black turtleneck sweater when doing so. But, the point that the competitive intelligence analyst needs to extract from this discussion is that economic webs contribute to increasing returns through the multiplication of value, the pairings of complementary offers, and the decrease of costs, lower unitary cost of buyer attraction. Economic web members generally contribute less in terms of resources to support their offerings and reap more comparative return than do sellers who operate outside of an economic web.

So, if an ecompetitor is participating in an economic web, either formally or informally, they can present a danger since their returns will be magnified and their costs will be minimized.

> *"How could this be a problem in a country where we have*
> *Intel and Microsoft?"*
> *Al "Let's Count All of the Dimples" Gore,*
> *Former U.S. Vice President*

Does the ecompetitor commoditize or differentiate their "informationalized" offering?

We discussed this previously, but let's just review it again before discussing commoditization and differentiation. Recall that what I mean by the informationalized product or service is the transformation of the benefits of an offering from their physical form to a form in which they are represented most completely as information. That transition of an offering is then represented electronically through sight and sound and purveyed, to the extent possible, through an ebusiness format such as a Web site. Let's return to the example of selling cars over the Web. Who would have ever thought that cars could have been sold in such a fashion? Before it happened, not many people, I'll bet. But let's look at it this way. A car is a collection of features. Those features can be represented as a list of information. Think about it. When you have gone somewhere to buy a car, whether that has been at a new or used car lot or in someone's driveway, you have asked the question, "What does it have in it?" The dealer or the owner then proceeded to rattle off a list of features or directed you to the sticker on the rear driver's side window. So when you are buying a car, like many other products and services, it simply becomes a collection of information points. Tinted windows, fuel injection, 16" wheels, bucket seats, driver's side air bag. You get the idea. The list can go on and on. Once the car's features have been listed, we get a very good idea of what benefits it can bring to us (Chuck thinks while shopping for new wheels, "Chicks really dig bucket seats.") or what problems it can solve for us (Sally ponders her budgetary shortfall. "Better mileage will help me make my rent," she thinks).

You know this is true. How many times have you bought a new car? Not a used car, a new car. And of those times, how many times did you actually test drive the actual car that you ended up owning? Not many I'll bet. You usually decide on the features, the salesperson let's you test drive a similar car, and then they wind up getting your actual car from another dealership or from the manufacturer. You often don't actually drive the car you have purchased until after you already own it. And that's because you buy a virtual car, a list of features, prior to taking delivery on the car that you drive home.

So if a product or service can be reduced to pieces of information which communicate benefit and problem solving, "informationalized" as in selling cars, the product or service can be more easily demonstrated to prospective customers. It, in essence, becomes a virtual product or service. Given some of the advantages of ebusiness, i.e., the mitigation of time and distance, these elements of a product can be represented virtually, at low cost, allowing for a large audience to be reached.

If, as a competitive intelligence analyst, you look at an ecompetitor and discover that they have been able to reduce their product or service to its essential benefit elements and have successfully represented those elements in an informational form, then they have succeeded in developing a virtual product. This virtual product can be digitized and transmitted through an electronic interface, with all of the implication of time and space mitigation and cost savings that that implies.

So, it seems that we have studied that concept of informationalizing and its inherent cost benefits somewhat thoroughly. Now, we need to move on from there and examine how the ecompetitor is using the informationalized offering, as a commodity or as a differentiated offering.

According to professor Michael Porter in *Competitive Strategy*, there are essentially three generic business strategies:[10]

- Cost Leadership or what has become known as Commoditization,
- Differentiation, or
- Focus, a combination of the previous two.

Commoditization. The competitor offers essentially the same product or service as other sellers, but it competes on price. The lowest prices usually win the business when using this strategic approach.

Differentiation. The competitor offers a product that is different from others in the marketplace and charges a higher price based upon the benefits brought by the differentiated features.

Focus. Combinations of commoditization and differentiation are used and applied in varying degrees to specific market segments.

Concerning the first two strategies, Porter outlines for each several skills and resources needed by the organization adopting each strategy. As the Focus strategy is a hybrid of the other two, he does not outline skills and resources in detail, saying only that combinations of those are applied in the Focus strategy. For our discussion, let's review the strategic support factors most pertinent to ebusiness competitive intelligence analysis. After each factor, we'll discuss why that factor is pertinent to the analysis of any ecompetitor.

Commoditization

- *Sustained capital investment and access to capital.*

  For an ecompetitor attracting customers through a low price, it is crucial to have ready access to capital, as low margins will cause a cash flow crunch. In the early days of dotcom pure plays, the access to capital was not a serious problem. However, after the April 2000 NASDAQ meltdown, ready access to capital markets has become a critical problem for most dotcom pure plays. For the ebusiness efforts running as divisions or subsidiaries of larger corporations, access to capital will probably be less of a problem. The analyst, once identifying an ecompetitor following a commoditization strategy and competing on price, must weigh the ecompetitor's ability to continue this strategy against its access to capital, defined, generally, by the criteria above.

• *Process engineering skills.*

Smaller ecompetitors selling commoditized product would have a greater tendency to outsource the manufacturing tasks to partners, purchasing manufactured goods for resale. In such a case, they would have little control over the manufacturing process and thus little control over costs. Larger ecompetitors would have a greater tendency to manufacture their own products, retaining cost control. The analyst must identify from where the products are coming in order to assess the likelihood of cost control and through it perpetuation of the low price, commoditization strategy.

• *Low-cost distribution system.*

Similar to manufacturing systems, small ecompetitors selling products often do not own their distribution systems. They "rent" them just like the manufacturing. Consequently, cost control is difficult, possibly impacting their ability to sustain the commoditization strategy. Larger ecompetitors more commonly have their own distribution system, allowing them to maintain a level of cost control. The analyst, again, must identify which commoditizing ecompetitor has the distribution cost control ability.

- *Structured organization and responsibilities.*

  A traditional system of management structure is what is indicated here, with all of the usual checks and balances on cost control. eCompetitors, large and small, often preferring to be seen as rebels, sporting titles such as Chief Marketing Guru or Primary Financial Potentate, are potentially less likely to follow "old fashioned" procedures of cost control. If the analyst can identify an ecompetitor with a loosely structured organization, it is somewhat likely that the ecompetitor may not maintain strict cost control, mitigating the efficacy of a chosen commoditization strategy.

Differentiation

- *Strong marketing skills.*

  This is where the informationalizing comes in. You probably thought I forgot about making that connection. Well, I didn't. I had to wait until we got to the differentiation strategy to talk about it because that is what informationalizing is all about. It's about converting the product benefit to an informational form such that the conversion communicates a differentiation in the product or service. Informationalizing only applies in the differentiation strategy, or in a related focus strategy. Informationalizing in the commoditization strategy is superfluous because there only the savings matter as the customer benefit, not the features. Thus, the analyst should assess only ecompetitors following the differentiation strategy for their ability to informationalize. The analyst may assess commoditization ecompetitors in informationalizing, but the conclusion should be that those ecompetitors are wasting their time.

- *Creative flair.*

  Naturally a creative flair is important when employing a differentiating strategy and doubly important when informationalizing. The analyst should be sure to assess the ecompetitor staff for its experience and expertise in creativity to be able to assess that ecompetitor's ability to succeed with its differentiation strategy.

- *Strong R&D and product engineering skills.*

  Naturally these skills will enable the ecompetitor to deliver on their differentiation promise. Skills such as these are often found more readily in larger organizations than in those that are smaller. The analyst should keep this in mind during assessment.

- *Corporate reputation for quality leadership.*

  Again, usually something present in the larger corporations rather than the dotcom pure plays which haven't been in business long enough to build a reputation for anything, despite how much they spend on advertising. eCompetitors which are divisions or subsidiaries of larger corporations may be able to benefit from the reputation of their older and more established parents. The analyst should therefore analyze differentiating ecompetitors to see if they have such a reputation onto which they may glom and to assess their level of success in informationalizing that reputation.

If B2B, does the ecompetitor have industry expertise, with which to forge relationships?

The competitive analyst reviewing business-to-business competitors must look at the background and expertise of the managers running the online effort.

Business-to-business, or B2B, commerce is a more complex process than business-to-consumer, or B2C, commerce. Some of the reasons for this complexity, inspired by the writings of consultant Walid Mougayar, are[11]:

- Large Transactions
- Credit Procedures/Payment Instruments
- Complex Needs/Wants & Relationships

Large Transactions. Companies purchase large amounts of almost any product or service that you can imagine. They buy these things either to resell or to incorporate into the product or service that they produce. Because they buy these things in large quantities the average value of the transactions usually exceed the average value of a consumer transaction.

Credit Procedures/Payment Instruments. Because the average value of these B2B transactions is so large credit and payment procedures often must be established between companies. Credit cards usually don't cut it here in B2B as they would in a B2C environment. The seller must have adequate assurance that they will receive payment for products purveyed or services rendered. To gain this assurance, B2B sellers require credit checks be made and payment terms outlined. This type of work is analog, requiring human interaction, adding imperfection, complexity, and cost to the creation of these procedures.

Although, as this book is written credit approval systems are being integrated into B2B sites so that credit approval on B2B customers is almost instantaneous after order entry. Thus, a move toward the elimination of the analog nature of B2B credit procedures is being taken. Yet, it will probably be some time until this newer digital credit procedure is fully enabled and running on a fair proportion of B2B sites.

Complex Needs/Wants & Relationships. Another reason for B2B complexity is that business-to-business needs and wants are often more detailed and specific than those of consumers. B2B customers often require that product or services adhere to a detailed list of specifications, accepting little variance in features. In order for B2B sellers to be successful, online or offline, extensive investigation must be made into their business customer requirements so that the product or service may be configured to meet the need. In order to accomplish this investigation, an in-depth knowledge of the industry is often required. Along with this expertise, relationships, or contacts, are often required to establish trust. These relationships and expertise are often the foundation of trust for meeting needs in a B2B transaction. Whereas trust in B2C markets is often established through brand names, brands are often not as important in B2B markets. The reason for this is that many B2B markets are fragmented, with many times the number of sellers that would appear in a B2C market. With so many sellers, brands are difficult to establish and have taken a backseat to the trust in known vendors.

B2C ecommerce efforts preceded B2B ecommerce efforts, putting, at least at this writing, the most ecommerce management experience available out there in the B2C field. This type of experience is not always directly applicable to a B2B marketplace. B2C relies heavily on brands. B2B does not. B2C does not rely on relationship building to the extent that B2B does. These vital differences in approach can give rise to problems for the B2B ecompetitor if and when they hire ebusiness management with a B2C background.

> *"Experience is the name everyone gives to his mistakes."*
> *—Wilde*

In doing a B2B competitive analysis, it is important for the analyst to identify any B2C consumer marketers or managers at the B2B ecompetitor. If former B2C managers are there in a great proportion, this will signal a weakness in terms of lack of business-to-business industry knowledge, expertise, and relationships,[12] the very factors upon which B2B trust is often based.

While looking for this weakness, the analyst should also look for a reciprocal strength, the presence of B2B management personnel who have an educational or vocational background in human behavior. As previously discussed, given that the B2B environment is so new, companies employing managers who understand the intricacies of human and social behavior will definitely have a competitive advantage over those ebusinesses not employing managers with the same skill sets. Skill such as these can be especially valuable in a B2B situation.

Does the ecompetitor cannibalize?

Oooh, yuck! This probably is not what you're thinking.

Cannibalization occurs when something eats its own. In business, this has traditionally referred to when a company comes out with a new product and its captures a significant portion of the market share of one of its other products. Cannibalization of a market has traditionally not been a smart idea, making this type of event mostly bad news for the cannibalizer/cannibalizee. Tradition says do not cannibalize. However, in the ebusiness era, you can throw the tradition out with your old sneakers because if you stand on tradition, you'll die from it.

For an effective ebusiness, here is how cannibalization may be structured to succeed. One of the most appropriate management theories I've seen in this area, and one that is applicable to ebusiness, is put forth by Harvard business professor Clayton Christensen.[13] He proposes that when organizations are faced with a technology that revolutionizes the way its products are made or its services are provided, the organization should move to incorporate that technology into its products or services through small divisions or subsidiaries. The reason, he says, for concentrating the new technology in a smaller strategic business unit is that, at first, the successes from the sale of the new technology are naturally expected to be small. If a large company, say a $500 million organization, commercializes the new technology with first year sales of say $1 million, then this sales level will seem insignificant to the large organization. However, Christensen suggests that if these sales are captured by a smaller subsidiary or division, starting at point zero, then $1 million in annual sales for the first year would be something that would likely be celebrated in a new unit, creating a sense of accomplishment, spurring employees on to more successes. By separating from the larger company, the new unit will also be isolated from the "good managers" of the bigger organization, whose responsibility it is, as Christensen suggests, to be good managers by maximizing shareholder value, eliminating proposals to move off into risky new ventures involving new technology. His theory continues.

His theory continues by saying that products containing new technologies should be aimed first at lower margin markets because the technology, being new, is likely to offer a lower quality product or service than that which it is replacing. The theory cautions that while this process may initially cannibalize the company's lower profit market segments, as the technology improves so will the product or service employing the technology. At that point, cannibalization may become complete, with the new technology assuming all of the former product's market share, including high margin segments along with the low margin segments. The theory also says that for companies to wait until the new technology reaches a "safe" level of market acceptance is suicide. By that time, early adopters will have perfected the technology and its purveyance, creating the so-called "first mover advantage," a significant competitive barrier.

Christensen does not attempt to apply this theory directly to ebusiness, yet I believe it is directly applicable. Certainly, ebusiness technology is a disruptive force in many industries selling either products or services or both. And because that technology may be assembled in such a way as to mitigate the problems of time and space, the technology can effectively offer a new type of product or service, possibly taking sales away from a company's existing physical world products or services. In recent years, we have seen many large companies, in B2C and B2B markets, splitting off their ebusiness efforts into smaller divisions or into completely independent subsidiaries in order to afford the new effort the best chance to grow, getting them away from the "good managers" of the larger entity. Through these independent business units, the precious first mover advantage can be created with cannibalization, in varying degrees, as a likely future occurrence.

The competitive intelligence analyst must realize that in certain ebusiness environments cannibalization is a smart move even if the cannibalizer takes in the short-term lower revenue or profits normally associated with a new technological offering that is regarded as lower in quality than its physical world companion. Doing so is better in the long run, rather than risking the total loss of revenue to a competitive ebusiness entrant.[14] Attending to this risk indicates that the competitor believes that ebusiness will become a dominant force in their industry. By splitting off a unit and going for cannibalization, the ecompetitor states that they believe doing so will allow them to gain a first mover advantage in the New Economy. Not attending to the risk, meaning not splitting off a unit, indicates their belief that ebusiness is of little consequence to their future.

Every competitive analyst needs to know the direction of its competitors and if that direction is taking the competitor in the direction of ebusiness, even at the price of cannibalization. Such a seemingly counterintuitive strategy could be highly dangerous to the analyst's company.

*   *   *

Marketing

Does the ecompetitor have connected customers and/or suppliers?

This question involves the ecompetitor's chief stakeholders and is obviously a basic issue. But again, just because it is basic doesn't mean that we should ignore it. If the ecompetitor is targeting customers or suppliers through its ebusiness effort and those parties are not connected through the proper electronic means, then they will not be able to transact business with the ecompetitor. End of story. This idea might seem like a no-brainer, but since some folks running ebusiness efforts today are a little light in the brains department, it should be something that the analyst should check out, just to cover the bases.

After looking at whether or not the targeted ecompetitors or suppliers can be connected, the analyst should go a step farther and look at the quality of the connection relative to the type of information being transferred over that connection as well as the viral nature of the content.

Connection Quality. Look at what type of market the ecompetitor targets. Is it B2B or B2C? If B2B, the question of connection quality is much less an issue than if the targeted market is B2C. Many companies are hooked into to the Internet by broadband connections such as T1, T2, or T3 lines. The quality of these connections is high, allowing the transfer of a great deal of data in a short period of time. However, if the competitor is targeting a B2C market, then the connection quality is more of an issue because most consumers have yet to experience broadband and are still connecting to the Internet over narrowband dial-ups.

If the competitive ebusiness is shoving large amounts of data through the pipe in the form of complex graphics or Java scripts, then this type of effort is best practiced in a B2B arena, rather than B2C. In B2C, narrowband access increases download time, giving rise to the expression the "World Wide Wait" from those consumers forced to wait for page loading, a situation not conducive to cementing lasting customer relationships.

Viral Nature. The competitive intelligence analyst should also examine the content sent to these connected customers or suppliers to see if it is "viral." The meaning here of the word viral is that information passed to one receiver contains a request or a reason for that receiver to pass it along to other receivers unknown to the original sender. The message then sent to a second or third receiver contains an identification, brand name or logo, from the original sender. The original sender then benefits by obtaining three receivers for the price of one. Remember increasing returns?

This viral nature of communication is peculiar to networks, which accelerate growth exponentially, organically; one turns into three and so on. Remember? Any sort of network can do this, but electronic networks are very good at performing viral communications quickly because they operate at the speed of light. So, if the ecompetitor has customers and/or suppliers connected via the Internet, the likelihood of that ecompetitor employing viral marketing tactics is very high, making for an element of danger to be experienced by the analyst's company.

Does the ecompetitor outsource to the customer?

This is an important aspect of ebusiness, enabling the customer to serve him or herself as much as possible. Why is it important? Oh come on, you should be getting this by now!

Per the "Killer App," outsourcing to the customer[15] means allowing and encouraging the customer to service its own account.

> *Outsource—Corporate jargon for securing services from outside the company*

Such tasks as checking on an order, changing an address, receiving payments, dispensing directions to an office, placing an order, or any one of the myriad pedestrian tasks completed by businesses daily are ripe for outsourcing to the customer. By doing so, the ecompetitor need not employ human labor to do something which can be accomplished by technology. In the long run, the technology is cheaper and the outsourcing shifts the cost away from the ecompetitor to the customer.

It is important for the competitive intelligence analyst to identify whether the ebusiness competitor avails itself of this potential cost shift. If the ecompetitor does this, then they are sharp, cool, and dangerous. And they probably encourage their employees to wear black turtlenecks. What is even more important here is that the analyst should identify whether the ecompetitor has made any arrangement for the customer to recoup some of the value of the cost shift. Let's say the ecompetitor provides facility for its customers to "serve" themselves online. The exact ways are many and varied, but are not important to this immediate discussion. What is important is that if the cost shift is made and the customer is not afforded the opportunity to capture an economic gain in the process, the customer, after a certain period of time, may become resentful, moving its business to another ecompetitor offering discounts or other accommodations to the customer in return for absorbing the shift.

Outsourcing to the customer identifies an ecompetitor that is formidable and one that is determined to reduce its cost curve through greater efficiencies. Such an ecompetitor realizes that customers like to save money and allows them to do so by performing some of the work. The Internet is particularly well suited to supporting this proactive position on customer relations. An ecompetitor operating in this fashion is not only reducing their own cost basis, but they are also increasing efficiency by decreasing the information asymmetry experienced by all customers everywhere, online or offline. This ecompetitor cannot obviously reduce information asymmetry everywhere, but they can contribute to its reduction in a small way by allowing customers to access and manage their own accounts. An ecompetitor acting like this can only benefit from its actions.

Is this type of ecompetitor dangerous to you? Come on, you should be getting this by now!

Does the ecompetitor target the right customers and meet their needs? If so, do those right customers include experimenters, convenience shoppers, and value shoppers?

Basically, the ecompetitor must target those customers hip enough to use ebusiness. Being still a technology in the early stages, only certain folks are going to patronize an ebusiness. The ecompetitor must realize this, as well as the competitive intelligence analyst reviewing that ecompetitor. The ecompetitor and the opposing analyst also must realize that what is being sold here is an offering. The ebusiness is selling more than just a product or a service. As previously mentioned, ebusinesses are also selling convenience, read that as timesavings. So, short of traditional target marketing to the needs that the products or services fill, the ecompetitor must additionally target those within the existing physical segment who will also use the ebusiness avenue to approach the ecompetitor.

In B2C, the ecompetitor must target those in its market segment who, to Michael De Kare-Silver, are known as[16]:

- Experimenters,
- Convenience Shoppers
- Value Shoppers, and
- Gen Xers.

Experimenters are, in standard marketing parlance, alternatively known as "early adopters" and will usually try anything new that a vendor has to offer provided the basic offering does satisfy a need or want. The experimenters are excellent targets for any ecompetitor. The reason for this is that even if the ecompetitor is selling an unexciting, boring old product, say bricks, the process used to sell that product is new. They're selling an offering, recall? And the process itself is part of the offering. The process saves time, and although it may not offer extrinsic cost savings, the process will definitely offer intrinsic savings. Such a situation will attract experimenters like flies on stink.

Convenience Shoppers, continuing from the previous thought, will definitely be great targets because of the timesaving involved.

The **Value Shopper** certainly qualifies as a prime target in ebusiness, as well. Because ebusinesses don't rely on physical plant to the extent of physical businesses, as well as for other reasons such as increasing returns, costs in ebusinesses can be less than those of their physical world counterparts. The timesaving factor provides intrinsic savings while the ability to outsource to the customer, per the previous discussion, provides the ebusiness with extrinsic cost saving. Through these mechanisms, the ebusiness can often afford to price its offering at a price lower than its physical world counterpart. For that reason value shoppers must be targeted by the ecompetitor.

Not withstanding the above three customer segment targets, the ecompetitor will want to target Gen Xers. This is important. Please underline the next two sentences. As mentioned in the Concepts section of this book, the Gen Xers are likely to be the most ebusiness friendly and savvy of ebusiness customers. An ecompetitor targeting members of that generation, whether for B2B or B2C, is likely to meet with a fair amount of success, adding to their danger.

In a B2C situation, the analyst should note that the ecompetitor would want to target all four of these segments. In a B2B situation, the ecompetitor will want to target all four, but with more emphasis on the convenience and value shoppers. The desire to target convenience and value shoppers within its normal market segment should be a concern because even though the B2B shopper is paid to perform shopping tasks, the B2B shopper, like most of us, probably feels overworked and does not want to waste a lot of time on things if they could be done more quickly. So, time-savings, convenience, would certainly be of interest to B2B shoppers. The value goal is very important for B2B shoppers because it's no tough bet to realize that B2B shoppers are charged with getting the best value available.

Thus, the competitive intelligence analyst should be alert as to whether the ecompetitor is positioning its offering for these customer segments and pursuing those segments aggressively. Doing so will make the ecompetitor a dangerous one.

Does the ecompetitor's offering rely on two key senses, sight and hearing, for promotion?

There are five human senses: taste, touch, smell, hearing, and sight. Some people say that there is a sixth sense, but until that is universally accepted, we'll stick with these. The Internet calls upon, primarily, only two senses, sight and hearing. There are some recent efforts as of this writing to make the smell sense relevant in the Internet mix, but the effort is rudimentary and does not impact the discussion of this issue significantly.

To judge whether an ecompetitor is either more or less dangerous on this issue is to assess the selection of senses through which the competitive offering must communicate.

The competitive intelligence analyst should endeavor to determine the degree to which the competitive offering relies on sight, hearing, taste, touch, and smell in developing customer interest in the offering. Since, online, only the senses of sight and hearing may be effectively employed, offering promotions relying on those senses are the only ones that, according to De Kare-Silver, have a good chance to be successful.[17] The other senses, taste, touch, and smell, may be significant in promoting certain offerings such as food, apparel, cosmetics, fragrances, and other similar consumer products, but they cannot, at the time of this writing, be effectively employed via the Internet. The analyst must consider these limitations when studying competitive B2C offers online. As for the analysis of B2B offerings, they will likely be less dependent upon taste, touch, and smell, so this should be considered when the effectiveness of online promotions in the B2B world are reviewed.

Thus, if the competitive intelligence analyst finds B2C competitive offerings based on attractions involving taste, touch, or smell, then it will be known that that ecompetitor will be a little less dangerous than perhaps previously thought. B2B offerings dependent on sight and sound only will be solidly grounded in an online environment.

How well does the ecompetitor help its customers to understand how the ecompetitor's offering helps the customer's business?

This discussion is limited to the B2B situation where communicating these benefits is vital to the ecompetitor's success. This issue, about which the competitive intelligence analyst should be aware, deals with how well the ecompetitor can communicate the benefits of its offering. Now, naturally this is crucial in an offline environment as well. But competitive assessment of the capability to communicate customer benefit is even more critical in the online environment just because so many more communication dimensions are available in the virtual world than in the physical world.

If a B2B vendor can demonstrate to a potential customer how their offering will help the customer's business or, taken one step farther, how their offering can, per Seybold, help the customer's customers,[18] then that B2B vendor will be a very effective communicator and one step closer to a sale. Not every B2B vendor can do this easily. Some cannot do it at all, while others do not even attempt to do so. For those that do attempt to reach this goal, though, the B2B vendor in the offline world will, as a first step, likely employ a written vehicle, a brochure, a letter, a postcard, or other similar communiqué. Online vendors may also use these tactics, in addition to using Web pages. When either does so, the B2B vendor uses only one sense, sight. A B2B vendor in the virtual world, of course, uses sight to demonstrate the offering, either through words and/or pictures but, as I mentioned in the discussion immediately preceding this one, in the online world the hearing sense through sound may also be exploited. Employment of the sound dimension in promotion is difficult, if not impossible, for the physical world B2B vendor to accomplish. Thus, the online vendor has an advantage over its offline counterpart, the transmittal of at least one more message, to be captured by one more sense. By doubling the number of senses addressed, more information may be imparted to and retained by the receiver, the goal of which is to demonstrate the advantage of the offering to the customer's business.

The ecompetitor may also use the online environment to communicate benefit to the customer's business through virtual modeling of a product, allowing the customer to see the features and benefits of different product combinations which the customer may assemble, virtually, on a Web site. For services, the ecompetitor may create a Web site that provides for "what if" analysis, another form of modeling, showing the customer the effects that the ecompetitor's service may have upon a customer business problem.

More dangerous than a physical world competitor? You bet.

Does the ecompetitor conduct Web-based market research?

What I'm talking about here is not the process of doing market research about general trends in ecommerce. What I'm talking about is how an ecompetitor gains feedback from its customers about the ease, or lack thereof, in using their ebusiness system. Some ebusinesses create a standardized system on their Web site in order to gain feedback in a systematic fashion. But, most ebusinesses do not do this. At best what most do is place a "Contact Us" link, usually buried at the bottom of the home page, so that customers can give feedback, if they want. Clicking on the link usually activates the clicker's email program. The guys in the black turtlenecks like to say "email client." It is then up to the clicker to compose a cogent message about their experience at the ebusinesses site. Take, for instance, the somewhat cogent message that I emailed around the time that I composed this section of the book. (This is an actual letter, but I have changed the names to protect those who are competitively Internet-challenged.)

From: Becker Research <Richard@xxxxxxx.com>
Date: Friday, July 14, 2000 9:10 AM
To: mail@xxxxxx.com
Subject: Hello Again

Hello Again Brudda,

Gosh. You guys don't make it easy to do business with you via the Web. This morning I emailed you to say that in wanting to send a Gen. Mac Nut gift basket, I visited your site. As the gift basket entries on your page did not list the contents I decided to take a pass. I preferred to know exactly what was in the basket before I sent it. Call me crazy, but, ya know, listing the contents of each basket, like you do in the catalog, isn't going to take much time.

I thought about this problem more as I slogged through my day. Mac nuts were calling me. And I just knew that the person to whom I wanted to send the gift, also heard the call. I wanted to fulfill their dream. But I thought, "No, those guys out there on the big island just make it too hard." So, I decided instead to go to the Smackin' Good Cakes site. You know, a little taste of Philly. (Or maybe you don't know.)

Anyway, I went to the Smackin' Good Cakes site. Their gift basket/box entries were nicely laid out, with a detailed listing of the contents. My informational requirements were met. I was ready to buy. I had my Visa in hand. As I pressed the Order button, I could hear the Philadelphia doo wop sound in my head. I could taste the bus fumes in their world famous hard pretzels available on every corner of the city. I was taken to the Order page. But alas. The order page was not secure. The page advised that for complete credit card security, I should print out the order form and fax it to them. Pish posh. Who could be bothered. With the taste of vanilla smackettes in my mouth, I dumped the site.

I thought vanilla smackettes are fine, but what my gift recipient really wants is mac nuts! They want to stuff their cheeks with those little reminders of Hawaiian heaven. I returned to your site. Deciding to give you one more try by getting a catalog and taking the slow route to Epicurean nirvana.

At your site, I clicked on the Print Catalog button. I filled out the form, dutifully and carefully. In anticipation, with my mouth watering for those mac nuts, I clicked the Submit button. Then I got an Error message saying the requested URL was not found on the server. "Oh, no." I thought. "How could these guys be so difficult to deal with? After all, they're Hawaiian. They're supposed to be laid back and accommodating."

Listen, guys. I'm a strategy consultant for ebusinesses. So I think I am qualified to say that you guys either don't know what you're doing with this Web site or perhaps it is that you just don't care about the Web site portion of your business. If it's the former, I can help. I'll be happy to take my fee in merchandise. If it's the latter, then it seems to me that you're making a big mistake because tourists from all over the world must be dying for a taste of your great merchandise after they return home. What a huge market you're missing. (Sorry. I neglected my flair for creative writing in this paragraph, but I had to hurry it up and get back to work.)

Take this as you will. Take this as you might. But, I hope you will improve so I can get some mac nuts to my friend without having to do cartwheels.

Mahalo,
Richard Telofski
Richard@xxxxxxx.com

This is a prime example of a competitor who, at least via their Web site, does not appear to be too dangerous.

From the context of gathering customer feedback, what has the company done wrong or done right?

Just read the email to find out. You're thinking. "What? Read the email. And parse all of this guy's gripes? That's too hard." No kidding. It is difficult. There are so many issues buried in that text that it is unlikely Gen. Mac Nut management will be able to easily isolate and extract them. Let's look at the issues, though. They were:

1. Perceived lack of ease in using the Web site.
2. Satisfaction with Gen. Mac Nut site being credit card secure.
3. Gen. Mac Nut product pages did not list the contents of the gift baskets.
4. Indirect competitive site, Smackin' Good Cakes, did list the contents of the products, the gift baskets.
5. Indirect competitive site was not credit card secure.

6. Indirect competitive site required extra work of customer in order to maintain credit card security.

7. Customer loyal and tries to overcome Gen. Mac Nut barriers by getting print catalog.

8. Technical glitch in the Gen. Mac Nut site when calling catalog-to-be-sent confirmation page.

Eight. Eight issues. Five of them either customer compliments or complaints and three of them complaints or compliments about an indirect competitor ebusiness approach. Those three about the indirect competitor are great competitor intelligence for Gen. Mac Nut.

Once Gen. Mac Nut got this email, they would have to have someone sit down, read it, and strip out the issues from the amusing writing. Maybe they would get all of the critical issues, maybe they wouldn't. Or maybe they would just chortle at the whimsical flair and flip the message into the old circular file on the way to their afternoon Kona coffee break. Who knows? Who cares? Gen. Mac Nut should care! They're missing the pineapple boat on this, brudda.

Brudda—Hawaiian accented
slang for the word
"Brother."

Remember the discussion on the value chain and how technology can be substituted for human labor in that chain. Well, customer feedback is part of the value chain. And if you have human labor stripping out feedback from customer emails, you're not using the ebusiness technological sense that was given to the human race to obsolete itself.

I know what you're thinking now. Did Gen. Mac Nut strip out these issues? Did they even answer? Yes. They answered. I suppose they didn't flip my message into the trash can, after all. But I didn't respond to ask them if they stripped out the issues. Why? Based on their response, I got the impression that they were just doing a "dust-off" and did no issue stripping. Here's what they said.

From: JayJac <jayjac@xxxxxxx.com>
To: Richard@xxxxxxx.com
Subject: Hello Again
Date: Fri, 14 Jul 2000 12:14:30

Richard,

Thank you very much for taking the time out discuss (sic) and critique our website. Unfortunately, I can't argue with many of your points, except to hope that you will be able (and willing!) to return to our website about the middle of August. At that point, we will have completed our re-launch, complete will (sic) all your favorite, mouth-watering macadamia products. And, we will even have our complete on-line gift catalog completed-which will include a description of each item in the basket/tower/tin!

Sorry we weren't able to accommodate you to your satisfaction this time. We definitely hope to be able to do better in the future.

Mahalo,
Jay Jack
V.P. Retail Operations

All he did was agree with me. Actually, he couldn't do much more because I had them dead to rights. But, give me a freakin' break. He didn't even offer to send me a print catalog! How hard would that have been?

Had this company been collecting customer feedback in an organized manner, they probably would have seen these problems coming and resolved them before they started. The system would have also been designed to spit out a print catalog, or at least an email back to the complainer for a snail mail address request. This type of automated response goes a long way to overcoming the imperfection of management oversights.

eBusiness systems are perfected for automated customer response mechanisms. What this implies is that ebusinesses may easily obtain formatted responses from customers so that the feedback may be, according to Seybold and professors Carl Shapiro & Hal Varian, easily fed into databases, parsed, organized, and analyzed.[19,20] Astute ecompetitors will follow this path, creating forms on their sites allowing customers to generate feedback on various topics. Those topics may be assigned value ranges using Likert scales or word groupings in a semantic differential approach. It doesn't need to be complicated, but it does need to be formatted. And, of course, an open text box can be made available for those gripes that just don't fit in the preformatted questions on the feedback form.

The point is that the dangerous competitor will provide facility for formatted customer feedback in the easiest manner possible for the customer. That ecompetitor will not require that customer to compose an email from scratch on their own email client. The formatted questionnaire will funnel the vital feedback into a form that can be quickly digested by management, taking the human element not completely, but mostly out of the process. The Web is perfect for this, the attainment of cheap, but valuable, market feedback.

If such a competitive ebusiness feedback system exists, the analyst can examine it, asking themselves if the system is intuitive and easy to use. The analyst must also ascertain whether the ecompetitor offers incentives for the completion of a feedback form, even if those incentives are small. Feedback encouragement devices such as discount "e-coupons" will go a long way in coaxing out that precious feedback from customers. The analyst should also not forget to determine if the request for feedback is strategically placed on the site, perhaps on the home page or on an order confirmation page, or if it is buried seven pages deep.

Can you imagine the uptick in Gen. Mac Nut's profit margin once they make that catalog easily obtained from a Web site visit? I can taste mac nuts now.

Does the ecompetitor produce lock-in for its customers?

If so, this is just a polite way of saying that the ecompetitor is "addicting" its customers to its offerings. That addiction may take the form of either an aesthetic differentiation or a certain price savings, or both. Remember? Differentiation or commoditization?

Loyalty programs with their accompanying discounts are, according to Shapiro & Varian, common examples of lock-in devices.[21] Offline companies had these devices long ago. Many have used them quite well. Frequent flier programs as well as supermarket savings programs proliferate. They are all created to produce lock-in. They all produce extra revenue for their creators. But with this upside there is also a downside. They all cost money to administer. They're a one-to-one relationship. No network effects or increasing returns to help defray the costs.

But in ebusiness, there is a unique type of loyalty program. What makes it unique is that it is created not only for the benefit of the ultimate customer, but also for the benefit of an intermediate "customer." That intermediate is called an affiliate.

Affiliate programs, because they depend on network effects and increasing returns, are easier and more cost effectively managed than their physical world loyalty program siblings. When these programs are in the hands of your ecompetitor, they become more efficient, and more dangerous to your company's survival.

As a loyalty program for affiliates, who would actually more properly be called sales agents, primary ebusinesses offer affiliate programs to secondary ebusinesses, i.e., the affiliates. The secondaries then publicize this relationship and link their ebusiness, mainly Web sites, to the primary ebusiness. Customers of the affiliate may buy from the primary through the link, affording the affiliate commission revenue. The primary ebusiness creates lock-in for the secondary, the affiliate, by offering cumulative payment plans, prizes, and other awards. The rewards are usually made on a cumulative basis, meaning that the more the affiliate sells, the higher the reward. This reward system is designed to prevent the affiliate from jumping ship and affiliating with another competitive primary ebusiness.

The analyst should determine whether its ecompetitor is the primary or the secondary in an affiliate program. If the primary, the ecompetitor presents a dangerous profile.

The danger is in the fact that through the affiliates the ecompetitor can reduce its marketing costs, drastically. After all, the primary ebusiness is just paying a commission to the secondary if and when a sale is made. There is no upfront cost to the primary. The secondary promotes and hosts the link, and spends money to do so.

What are the ecompetitor's customers' switching costs?

OK. So there are locked-in customers. Seemingly. But as Lawrence of Arabia said in the movie of the same name, "Nothing is written." There may be a way to get those customers, either affiliates or the all important ultimate customer, away from the ecompetitor and into your fold. The surest way to finding out is by examining their switching costs.

What are switching costs? These are the implicit and explicit costs incurred when a customer changes over to another supplier. Naturally that customer wants to eliminate switching costs. In doing so, the customer wants to receive back benefit that exceeds the cost of their switching. For the analyst to identify the level of benefit needed to get that customer to switch, they must first identify criteria that attract customers to the ecompetitor. Such criteria, as suggested by Porter and Shapiro & Varian, may consist of:[22]

- product or service quality,
- brand recognition and trust,

- convenience, and
- cost savings

over competitive offerings. The analyst must put a value on each criterion. The analyst's company must then construct an offering that increases the value of each criterion so as to move the customer away from the competitive offering. In other words, to steal the customer that customer's switching costs must be returned, at a premium, to that customer when it purchases a competing offer. The analyst's company must also be sure that the revenue received from the customer covers not only the customer's switching costs but the company's switching costs, i.e., the expense required to attract the customer away from the competitor, as well.

Product/Service Quality. The offering quality may be vulnerable in terms of the way the offering is delivered. If a product is being sold, the core product itself may be subject to little quality variation due to standard manufacturing methods. However, the larger product, the offering as defined earlier, may have some competitive weakness. One weakness of that offering could be delivery time, complicated by fulfillment systems that the ebusiness competitor has not as yet perfected. Such is a common weakness among many ebusinesses as they often outsource their fulfillment function or experience demand in excess of the capacity of their internal system.

Fulfillment—Warehousing, logistics, distribution of product.

Brand Recognition. Another weakness along switching cost criteria could be brand recognition, communicating trust. In the present stage of ebusiness, brand recognition is extremely important. As with well-known brands in the physical world, the well-known online brand implies to the customer that their order information will be handled confidentially and accurately and that the offering will arrive as promised. Not every ebusiness competitor can accomplish this, and the ones that do are usually the better known brand names in their industry. If the ecompetitor does not have an adequate brand image established, then the competitive intelligence analyst's company, depending on the level of their own brand image, may be able to pick-off some of the ecompetitor's customers.

The competitive intelligence analyst must also be alert for a situation that could neutralize the value of brands in ebusiness. This has nothing to do with competitors and everything to do with technology.

As of this writing we are not yet there, but in the near future infomediaries could negate the need for a brand to communicate offering features and pricing, i.e., the value ratio. Often persons use brand image to assess the value relationship, the proportion of benefit derived from an offering's necessary cost. In using infomediaries, potential customers will be able to easily, and conveniently, search offerings along specific features and prices. As was stated earlier, after infomediaries are a common tool used by all sorts of buyers, there will be no more hiding behind brand images. Buyers everywhere, B2C or B2B, will gain new power. Offerings will truly need to rely on their strengths and withstand the test of efficient search processes, more efficient than a person could accomplish alone without this technology.

"Truth is the safest lie."—*Yiddish Proverb*

Convenience. A weakness in the area of convenience is also something to which the competitive intelligence analyst should attend. Based on the content and functionality tests mentioned earlier in this chapter, the analyst should check the convenience of use of the competitor's ebusiness effort for its targeted customers. eBusiness is about convenience. If it's inconvenient, prospective customers are likely to say bye-bye prior to even becoming customers.

Cost Savings. The issue of weakness along the cost savings switching criteria can be one of debate. In some ebusiness markets, where their participants are following a commoditization strategy, price differential will be a guiding criterion for deal-seeking customers. Companies will need to work hard to reduce price, mitigating switching costs for potential customers. But in other markets, where differentiation is the pre-dominant strategy, it is known that pricing is not one of the most important criterion, and that cost savings as a switching cost can be overshadowed by convenience and ease of ebusiness use.

If the competitive intelligence analyst can identify which of these criteria, or other significant criteria, are the most important to potential customers in the industry under study, then plans can be made to reduce the switching costs and humble that dangerous ecompetitor.

Are there contractual commitments between your ecompetitor and any of its customers?

Contractual commitments are likely to occur in a B2B situation. Business interactions live on contracts. Normally, when companies make exchanges, they won't lift a finger until they have it all down on paper. This is so in the offline economy and in the online economy. It's a bit odd to be so dependent on paper in this online economy, isn't it? Contracts would be rather unlikely in a B2C arrangement. That's not to say that they don't happen. They just don't seem to be nearly as frequent.

An example of a B2B arrangement where there would be a contract would be with a marketplace Web site selling commoditized items like steel, chemicals, and industrial supplies. With many such Web sites, customers and suppliers have set out contractual terms for supply, delivery, credit terms, and other parameters, using the Web site as a convenient interface, a virtual market.

Per Shapiro & Varian, lock-in of this type[23] is usually long-term and difficult to break. Here, as in most business definitions, "long-term" means in excess of 366 days. The party attempting to lure the customer out of the contractual arrangement would not only need to entice the customer along the switching cost criteria discussed earlier, but would also need to cover any penalty the customer would incur for abrogating the contract. Such penalty is likely to be substantial. This substantial penalty would make securing the customer's business a daunting task indeed.

So, guess what? As a competitive intelligence analyst, if you encounter an ebusiness contractual arrangement, the most practical thing that can be done is try to determine the length of the contract, its renewal date, and alert your management to knock on the customer's door prior to the renewal date. Prudent. Measured. Reasonable. And your management will probably agree, unless they're a bit daft, that this would be the best course of action.

> *"A verbal contract isn't worth the paper it's written on."*
> —*Samuel Goldwyn*

Does the ecompetitor require specific training for customers to use or to get the offering?

If the answer to this one is yes, do a happy dance. Why, you say? You think this is bad because it locks in that potential customer for the ecompetitor. Hah! Wrong you are. Read on.

As in the contractual commitment discussion above, if this situation occurs at all, it would most likely take place in B2B. Specific training may be necessary where a vendor and customer have a complex interface set up, requiring knowledge of different purchasing or specification procedures depending upon the product or service to be purchased.

Such a requirement for specific training would seemingly be a probable method of lock-in employed by the ecompetitor. But in reality, a good ebusiness system would minimize the need for specialized skill and training in order to use the system. A good system would encourage ease and openness. If anything, the requirement of specialized training would tend to repel customers, signaling a weakness. This weakness is one which the competitive intelligence analyst would bring to the attention of its management so that arrangements could be made to exploit that weakness through the creation of a simpler system requiring only the brains of a chimp to operate.

Is the ecompetitor's ebusiness system open or proprietary?

This concept is what I was laying groundwork for in the previous discussion. The necessity of special training creates an atmosphere of exclusion, one that dictates that only certain people, or chimps, can operate that system. Such a posture is not conducive to enlisting as many customers as possible. Why make it difficult for them to get to you? Special training closes the system on which the seller wants as many people as possible.

This concept of open and closed systems is what led to one of the chief differences between the DOS/Windows® and Apple® operating systems.

Apple, at the beginning, refused to open their operating system to computer makers other than Apple so that the system could be used to run non-Apple computers. The DOS/Windows folks realized a better way in that they could leverage the value of PCs made by others by allowing for openness, and licensing the DOS/Windows system to any computer maker. Of course hind site always being 20/20 or better tells us that the DOS/Windows people were more successful. But ditch the hindsight. *Why* was DOS/Windows more successful?

DOS/Windows was more successful because of its openness. Well, of course, openness could be called a relative term. Some folks may not consider the people who bring you Windows to be very open, especially after the anti-trust trial events of 2000. But the Windows® folks were open in the sense of allowing their systems to be used throughout the industry and in allowing other products to be created for Windows, each of whose offerings contributes more economic value to the offerings of other Windows system participants than if those offerings were unavailable. Remember? Economic webs? That's what Bill (Gates, not Clinton) and Company created, whether or not they were aware of what it was called at the time we'll never really know. But it doesn't matter if they knew the name of it or not. They knew that the concept was explosive and through it they became dangerous competition. Really dangerous. And the Steves, Wozniak and Jobs, felt the pain in their more proprietary system.

That was back in the dark ages, the 1970s and 1980s, before the Internet became something about which we grew tired of hearing. As the PC days became more mature, we grew to like systems that would help us interchange information, easily, quickly, without needing a degree in software engineering. We started to exchange information via floppy disk exchange, via tape exchange, then via CD exchange, and then via telephone over DOS® based electronic billboards. There were sometimes problems. Disk or tape formats weren't always compatible. Special software was needed to dial-up billboards. We liked being "connected," rudimentary as it was. But we ached for more, to be set free from the proprietariness which threatened our informational freedom. Then came the Web, the first real common denominator of the Internet. In 1994, the first real year of the Web, it was painfully apparent that in the Internet age proprietary ebusiness systems just wouldn't cut it. Here's why.

Do you know from where the "Inter" prefix of Internet came? The Internet started out as a collection of networks, some public and some proprietary. The proprietary portions tended to slow things down and just made the whole system cumbersome. Eventually, the owners of the proprietary systems realized that they were bogging things down. But, they weren't being altruistic when they decided to open up their systems to public interchange. They realized that by opening their systems they would become more valuable because more people could use them. They started to obey, unwittingly, something that came to be known as Metcalfe's Law. Robert Metcalfe, one of the founders of 3Com®, said that the value of a network increases by the number of users of the network, squared. So, every time a new user comes aboard a network, the value of the network to all participants increases exponentially. Remember increasing returns?[24]

EDI, electronic data interchange, which is believe it or not still used today, is a proprietary system, one that can be accessed only by subscribers. EDI is used as an electronic interface between vendors and customers. This technology was created in the pre-Internet explosion. The Internet did exist when EDI was born, but it hadn't made it to common usage yet. But because EDI is restrictive in the number of participants it accommodates, EDI retards the forces that drive Metcalfe's Law to increase the value of the system.

As the Internet broke into the collective human consciousness and as systems were invented to make Internet access easy, the Internet started to connect not only the public networks but those private networks as well. The Internet truly became "Inter," which as defined by Webster is a prefix meaning "between," "among," or "together." The Internet became the uniting force among all of those networks, linking them together for the most public use possible, opening access, increasing value, making our lives better.

This is not to say that all information obtainable through the Internet is public. Oh, heck no. Obviously this is not the case. Information is best obtained through an open system like the Internet, but some of it is best secured by password and firewall for only those authorized to use it.

So what does this entire long, but entertaining and enlightening, discussion mean to the competitive intelligence analyst? The intent of this discussion is to provide the analyst with background information on the value of open systems. In *The Third Wave*,[25] Toffler called an open information transfer system a necessity for an information economy. This understanding will help the analyst to realize that an ecompetitor using a closed, proprietary system, one requiring special equipment or procedure, is not dangerous. In fact, that ecompetitor would be a pigeon, one easy to pick off, clean. For an ecompetitor to be truly dangerous, a basic requirement is that they operate on an open standard, one that supports actions that provide exponentially increasing returns.

Is most of the ecompetitor's promotion online?

This is where a lot of ebusinesses go way off track. So far off track that they're almost running completely out of the stadium. It seems that they figure that since they exist online, they should promote exclusively online. Hello? Think about it. Where do you spend most of your time?

If you're not an Internet junkie and you're over the age of reason with a steady job, then you probably spend most of your time offline. Most people, at least at the time of this writing, spend the majority of their waking hours offline. But who knows? All of that could change in the future. For right now, during that time people do things like eating, cutting the grass, working offline, and attending to offline media such as radio, newspapers, television, and magazines. We can't all be staring into the computer screen all the time. If we did, the eye doctors would be making more of a fortune than they already are.

Doesn't it make sense that an ebusiness competitor should spend more to promote offline than online? Generally, I would say yes. What would you say? Of course, there are exceptions. There are exceptions to almost anything. But if I addressed each exception individually, you would have had to buy this book in about 47 volumes. Let's stick to the big picture.

The competitive intelligence analyst should check its ecompetitor's spending on promotion. Such figures on offline spending for many American companies are readily available, most popularly from a Manhattan based outfit called Competitive Media Research, or CMR. They track a lot of offline media spending by public and private companies. The chances are good that they're going to have some dish about how your chosen ecompetitor burns its offline media money. There are other similar companies that track online spending so you should be able to get an accurate picture as to what proportion of your ecompetitor's promo buck is going virtual and what proportion is going physical.

If you see an ecompetitor whose online spending is over-the-top and seriously outweighs offline spending, do yet another happy dance because you'll know you've got one who's not dangerous. In fact, this is the mark of an ecompetitor that is downright weak and guilty of sloppy marketing. This situation is analogous to overweighting a stock portfolio in favor of one stock; it may pay off, but it's a risky way to live. If your research tells you your ecompetitor has a more balanced approach between offline and online promotion, then you'll have an ecompetitor that is more dangerous than one who concentrates the promo in the virtual world only.

Is the competitive ebusiness effort promoted as the business itself or is the ebusiness effort a promotional tactic for a physical business?

This is a clear indicator of competitive strategic direction. The competitive intelligence analyst should identify this direction early on in the ecompetitor examination.

The analyst should determine if the competitive ebusiness is the center of offline and online promotional efforts. In other words, look to see if the ecompetitor is trying to drive potential customers to its Web site. If so, the ecompetitor's strategic choice is clearly toward the virtual realm. They will pursue all the advantages of an ebusiness, increasing returns, mitigation of time and space, etc., putting them on a different competitive level from physical firms and making them, because of the cost saving aspects of ebusiness which we have previously discussed, highly dangerous.

If the ebusiness competitor uses its Internet presence as a purely promotional vehicle, driving customers to the physical outlets of its business, then the ecompetitor is choosing to remain in the physical realm and will present a far less dangerous profile than one opting for cyberspace as its home.

Are the ecompetitor's offline and online promotional efforts integrated?

This is one of the hardest tasks for most ebusiness efforts. Often, regardless if the company is a pure play or a click & mortar, an ebusiness will do at least some offline and some online promotion.

Click & Mortar—An ebusiness
inside of a physical world company.

Many ebusinesses will at least try to show some common sense by not overweighting their promotional portfolio in favor of any promotion avenue. What usually happens with many ebusinesses is that the online and offline promotional programs will have some differences between them. What kind of differences? Often inconsistent look, such as not including a brand logo, celebrity or character representative, or common color scheme. Why do they make these dumb integration mistakes? The reason is often because there are two different advertising agencies working, one online and one offline. Often, agencies don't have expertise in both areas, so the responsibilities must be split. And frequently agencies, being competitors themselves, don't like to coordinate with other client agencies. So, things fall through the cracks as the client's advertising director tries to catch them with a mitt that's too small.

Competitively, this lack of promotion integration can indicate that there is a good chance that the audience will not relate an ecompetitor's offline message to its online message. The audience may feel that the two messages are from different companies, splitting the ecompetitor's advertising effectiveness, effectively doubling the cost of the advertising. Guess what this does to their presence in the marketplace? Yeah. It makes them less dangerous to your company, provided your company is not making the same boneheaded mistake.

The crossmedia integration of promotional efforts, either by the ebusiness competitor alone or in conjunction with a marketing partner, represents, according to Seybold, a formidable one-two punch across different promotional levels, the real and the virtual.[26] Now, by real I mean print, broadcast, direct mail and other conventional means. By virtual I mean banner ads, email, text ads, interstitials, and other promotional devices employed via the Internet. The ecompetitor that is able to integrate all of the different tactics has many more chances for exposure than does the ecompetitor using only one avenue or using both avenues in such a way that one cannot be connected in the mind of the audience to the other.

Is the competitor's pricing self-adjusting, i.e., market responsive, auction-based?

Previously we discussed fractals and interactivity as two basic concepts in ebusiness. Some people freak out when cerebral notions like fractals are bandied about. But please remain calm. It's not hard to understand the character of fractals if you have a good, simple explanation. And here it is.

We said that a fractal system is one that has the same nature and form at every level of the system. We also said that the economic system, as a fractal, should allow for the interaction of supply and demand forces at every level of the system just as it does at the system's macro level. Also discussed was interactivity, the possible process of all participants in the system sending messages to each other.

Knowing these concepts as key to an ebusiness system, the competitive intelligence analyst should be on the alert for competitive efforts allowing for dynamic pricing interaction by customers. This situation often takes the form of an auction mechanism where an ecompetitor may sell offerings to the highest bidder. Or conversely, the ecompetitor may take part in a reverse auction where it is a buyer and has suppliers bid on its business by offering progressively lower prices.

Either of these auction approaches leverages the efficiencies of supply and demand interaction, bringing the benefits experienced at the macroeconomic level right down to the microlevel. Not only are pricing efficiencies experienced, but the ecompetitor also has the built-in ebusiness advantage of the time and distance defeating tool of Internet interactivity, increasing the number of participants on both sides of the supply and demand equation. These are formidable combinations which are dangerous to competitors. These combinations are dangerous to competitors because they change the nature of the way information is obtained and upon which it is acted, accelerating the pace of business, and satisfying customers as a result.

Does the ecompetitor make a lower price available online due to reduced cost structure?

Making offerings available at a lower price online would be valid issue of exploration for ecompetitors selling the exact same offering online as well as offline. This issue applies to ecompetitors following either the commoditization or the differentiation strategic form. The competitive intelligence analyst should study the ecompetitor's offering to determine: 1) whether the online and offline offerings are exactly the same; and, 2) whether there is a pricing difference between the offline offering and the online offering. Because of the reduced cost structure achievable online, the common expectation seems to be that the online offering should be priced lower than the offline offering.

The pricing of an offering online at the same price as an identical offering offline certainly spells competitive weakness. As you'll recall we previously discussed ecompetitors that outsourced to the customer and how they will allow the customer to recoup some of the cost shift. One powerful way to do this is through a lower price. In general, in my opinion any ecompetitor that does not price an identical offering lower online than offline is not dangerous at all and, in fact, quite stupid.

*　　　　*　　　　*

Management & Organization

How flat is the ecompetitor's organization? Do employees have access to customer information?

As I pointed out earlier, another of the advantages of ebusiness is its inherent, cost-effective ability to collect information about the customer and to provide that information to all employees throughout the company. A result of this advantage is that the ebusiness, per Downes & Mui, requires fewer layers of employees between the customer and top management than does its physical world cousin.[27] Technology supplants labor. The existence of a sophisticated network within in the ebusiness enterprise increases the efficiency of the overall system, i.e., the company. No surprise.

> *Flat Org—The Catholic Church*
> *has only five layers of*
> *management between*
> *the top guy and the "customer."*

Also remember from our discussions that the free flow of information at the macroeconomic level is what allows the economy to move toward efficiency. Of course, we actually never reach the optimum level of efficiency because of information asymmetry, but human beings being what we are, we constantly strive for it. Also recall the idea that at the microeconomic level, the interaction within companies virtual and physical alike, a free flow of information is not always necessarily the case. Information often does not flow as freely within a company as it does outside a company. The reason for this is, at least partially, as I previously stated is the desire for political control of information by management.

> *"One of the penalties for refusing to participate in politics is that you end up being governed by your inferiors."—Plato*

By its control of information, management thwarts the fractal nature of the overall system. Davis & Meyer explored this in *Blur*. Such a situation disallows maximum information use toward company benefit through employees empowered to make the company work. One can only hope that this practice is inadvertent and not a conscious effort to subvert the forces of nature. But I fear it isn't. I believe this practice to be a subversion, resulting in an internal friction, impacting the efficiency of the enterprise, and interfering with the company's ability to interact efficiently with the macroeconomy right outside its door.

In the case of an ebusiness, where technology supplants labor, allowing for fewer employees, and causing those employees to be closer to the customer, internal friction can be detrimental, if not downright fatal, to the survival of the enterprise. Normally, online businesses are organized to provide employees more power in decision-making, since they are, because of the intervention of technology, closer to the ultimate customer than they would be in a physical company. This mitigation, or ideally the elimination of internal friction, requires a new mindset, one very different from that experienced in physical companies run by risk averse management.

This New Economy mindset seeks to establish a competitive advantage through the empowerment of and faith in employees. In 1999 and 2000, Internet companies drew thousands of new hires away from traditionally structured physical world companies, where the hierarchy keeps most employees away from the customer. One of the reasons for the attraction to Internet companies was the allure of stock options and, through them, instant riches. The seemingly liberal award of stock options to a large proportion of Internet company employees does not indicate a desperation to attract employees. Quite the contrary, at the time of the stock option mania Internet companies had little trouble in attracting new hires. I believe that this practice indicates an Internet company core belief. A belief that since their employees, being closer to the customer, could more directly affect the outcome of their company than can their counterparts in a physical world company, those employees should rather be managed as "partners" with the awarding of stock options acting as a "partner management" mechanism.

This new form of employee/partner management ultimately can lead to more ideas from the employees about how to make the business better for customers. The improvements lead to more revenue, then to employee recognition and rewards, to more ideas, and so on. This growth of ideas and subsequent improvement become exponential and one feeds upon the other. The result of this new management mindset is that the ebusiness enterprise while following this paradigm establishes a competitive advantage that is hard for competitors to copy. Where technological processes or marketing methods are created to establish competitive advantage, that advantage can be fleeting, and disappear as soon as the technology or marketing approaches can be copied by competitors.

However, the adoption of a new management mindset, one where faith in employees to do the right things pervades all levels of the organization, is not as easily created by competitors, representing a formidable competitive advantage.

> *"Let the people think they govern, and they will be governed."*
> *—Penn*

This type of competitive advantage is achievable through the employment of an ebusiness system replacing inefficient layers of human labor. The organizational result is a flattened structure relative to the physical company counterpart. The free flow of information enabled by ebusiness system supports the new mindset and vice versa.

If your intelligence gathering finds that the ecompetitor is relatively flat and light, with a vast array of internal information available to all-level employees empowered to act in the best interests of the customer, then watch out. Do not do your happy dance. You have a dangerous competitor, one with employee/partners who are compensated to make a difference.

Is the competitive ebusiness effort just a small unit of a larger brick & mortar? Or is it a full-fledged Internet pure play?

This is a basic question. But don't let its elemental nature throw you off and cause you to ignore this issue. Knowing the answer is important. Internet pure plays usually act differently than small ebusiness units packed within a larger physical world company.

Pure plays by their very nature are more risky. They are operating in a completely new and untried environment. They are pioneers. They have no road map. So, because of the circumstances in which they find themselves, they must take more risks, act more impulsively and unpredictably. Impulsive and unpredictable movements tend to make companies more dangerous competitors.

Different from a pure play is a small ebusiness unit inside a brick & mortar operation operating in tandem with the physical company. This is called a "click & mortar." Because the ebusiness effort is housed within the management structure of the physical company, the click & mortar will likely be subjected to management and budgeting whims of the predominantly physical business. In all probability, as Christensen suggests,[28] the "good managers" of the established physical world business won't really give the click & mortar the room it needs to grow. That click & mortar will, even if inadvertently, adopt to a degree the parent's management style and risk profile, making for a somewhat more subdued rival. The ebusiness effort that is budgetarily constrained and not allowed to provide for a flatter organization augmented by the free flow of information at the lower levels has the odds stacked against it. Often, click & mortar operations fall into this category.

This is not to say that a pure play is a more formidable competitor than a click & mortar. Pure plays often have more financial problems which can restrict competitive strengths. This is to say that the competitive intelligence analyst must be aware of these issues so as to be able to identify the willingness of pure plays to assume large risks and the problem of physical world company management influence on click & mortar operations as competitive factors to be examined.

How many people work for the competitive ebusiness effort?

Knowing this was important in the days of physical world competitive research, but it's so much less important today, that the question should not even be considered as critical.

With today's ecompetitors, where matter doesn't matter, where organizations are flat, where outsourcing is done to customers and corporate partners, where technology supplants human labor, the number of people employed by an ecompetitor just isn't relevant to a competitive analysis.

How are the competitor's people organized? That is, how many marketers, technicians, financiers, etc.

Knowing this would give you a general indicator of just where they think their distinctive competence is.

eBusiness companies are either marketing or technology driven. They're definitely not ace financiers. Hey! With all of the attention on dot com stocks, why do I say that?

There is relatively little financial management skill required in the type of financing supporting most dot coms.

*Dot Com—American slang
referring to Internet
pure play companies.*

They take their marketing or technology idea to venture capitalists or to angel investors, show how the idea can capture gobs of market share, and the money guys and gals throw pesos at them. Well, it's not quite that easy. But the point is that ebusinesses rarely have sharp financial wizards in their office, calculating the nuances and effects of internal versus external funding in the same way as offline financial officers. Why? Well quite simply, most of them start off with a pile of cash, usually an equity play, and then they're on their own. They run that cash down, this is called the "burn rate," until the business model proves itself, the company closes its doors, or some other fool acquires them or gives them more equity interest. There is no internal financing to compare to external financing because they have very little revenue compared to expenses. Thus, no pesky internally generated funds to worry about. This burn-the-equity approach, unfortunately found all too often in ebusiness, simply supports bad marketing programs or technology about which the marketplace remains unmoved.

If the ecompetitor appears heavy in the marketing staff, you'll know that they're going for the glitz and the glamour and that they are probably dressing up a less than riveting idea based on a weak or average technology. If the ecompetitor appears heavy in the tech department, this could indicate that they're a bit more of a formidable competitor. Usually technologies that last have proved to be special and more competitive than marketing fluff wrapped around a so-so technology. But keep in mind what was discussed previously about the maintenance of competitive advantage. Truly sustainable competitive advantage in ebusiness comes from neither marketing nor technology. Rather it comes from the empowerment of and trust in all employees who are all placed close to the customer. So if you find a technology heavy ecompetitor, check out their technology to see if it solves a customer problem and also check out the way their employees are organized to work.

"Systems die; instincts remain."—O. W. Holmes, Jr.

Is the ecompetitor organized for global expansion?

Concerning international expansion, one thing that the competitive intelligence analyst needs to look for is how the ecompetitor has its resources structured. In order to be a dangerous competitor, the ecompetitor should have the following functions centralized: business strategy, leadership, human resources, marketing services, and infrastructure management. Regionalized functions, per Sawhney et. al., should be marketing management, purchasing, logistics, industry expertise management, and business development (partner procurement).[29]

The reason why these functions should be organized this way is so that the ebusiness may get the most bang for its buck. Duh! Let me explain.

The functions of business strategy, leadership, human resources, marketing services, and infrastructure management should be centralized because these are activities that have relatively little international variation and thus may be managed across various national and cultural boundaries. With input from local management, central management may operate these processes in a somewhat standardized fashion, allowing for economies of scope and cost containment.

The function of marketing management locally enables the ebusiness to decide better what to offer in various foreign markets and how to offer it. Purchasing and logistics seated locally allow the ebusiness to secure the best deals available in local supplies and services and, from a marketing perspective, communicate to customers that the ebusiness is committed to local businesses and is not just a foreign carpetbagger. Industry expertise should be local because, obviously, there can appear great variations in business procedures, even within industries, as business migrates from one country to the next. Local management best serves business development because it allows the ebusiness the opportunity to identify the best partners available within a national market and strike a partnership as an equal business within that country.

If the ecompetitor does not adhere to this basic model, they will probably be inefficient in their approach to global expansion. This implies a higher cost profile than necessary, a competitive weakness.

Is the ecompetitor's ebusiness model transportable globally?

There are three basic elements to any ebusiness model. They rely on the movement of:

- information,
- money, or
- products

or any combination of the three.[30] The competitive intelligence analyst needs to examine its ecompetitor to identify how many of the three are being moved.

Information. The movement of information is basic to any ebusiness and relies on a sound telecommunications infrastructure that must exist in order for the ecompetitor to be successful. Of course, the analyst must also examine whether or not the ecompetitor's targeted market segments have easy and inexpensive access to the telecommunications network. Provided that access is available, if the ecompetitor is simply moving information, like a portal would, then the ecompetitor may apply its business model in many different foreign markets.

Money. If the ecompetitor's ebusiness relies on the movement of money, then there must be some type of electronic friendly payment system in place within the national market that the ecompetitor wishes to penetrate. The competitive intelligence analyst must consider how the ecompetitor will deal with currency conversion, tax issues, and credit card payments and decide if this competency is already in the ecompetitor's business model prior to international expansion. Additionally, the analyst must consider the state of credit card usage within certain national markets and if that is a viable payment alternative for potential customers of the B2C ecompetitor. If it is a B2B effort that the analyst is studying, then research must be performed concerning the ability of the ecompetitor to transfer its type of pre-negotiated payment and fulfillment systems to the national markets of interest. The analyst should also determine if the B2B ecompetitor has employed one of the online B2B credit approval systems that are being developed at the time of this writing. Of overall consideration here would be whether there are cultural differences among markets that would prevent the money movement processes from being deployed.

Products. If the competitive ebusiness relies on the movement of physical goods, the analyst must examine the ecompetitor's distribution system. If the system is locally based, as suggested above, the ecompetitor will enjoy some strength in this area. However, the analyst must study that system for quality and compare it to other systems to be employed by the ecompetitor in other national markets. Of question here would be whether the same type of delivery methods and warehouse systems exist in targeted foreign markets as already exist in the ecompetitor's currently occupied markets.

If the analyst finds that the ecompetitor has a sound process supporting one or more of the ecompetitor's chosen basic elements, then the ecompetitor may transport its business model internationally in order to preempt competition local or foreign in nature. The ecompetitor may transport this model in two ways: frontal assault or infiltration.[31]

Frontal assault is to attempt to open for business in a foreign region, e.g., Western Europe. Infiltration is to attempt to establish several footholds in small portions of larger regional markets, e.g., a single country or section of Western Europe or Latin America. What the analyst must be alert for is if the ecompetitor has chosen a frontal assault strategy, then the analyst must determine if the area is relatively homogenous in terms of culture, consumption, business procedures, and customer behavior. Only through this homogeneity will the competitive ebusiness effort survive. If the ecompetitor has seemingly chosen an infiltration strategy applied in many places at once, then the analyst must look to determine if the targeted areas are mutually homogenous. In all likelihood, they will be quite diverse. The heterogeneity does not indicate a problem to the competitive ebusiness provided the business model is confined to the transfer of information, such as a portal.

Regardless of whether the ecompetitor moves information, money, or product, or any combination of those three, any ebusiness effort wanting to go international must realize that foreign languages need to be employed in order to be successful. Statistics and common sense tell us that as Internet usage spreads across the world's population, the English language will decreasingly become the primary language of the average Internet user. At this writing, current statistics from various sources say that over half of Internet users are English speakers. But those same statistics forecast that by 2005, much less than half of the Internet users will be English speakers. The ecompetitor that positions now for a multi-language capability will be in a position to capture a larger global market share later and will be a truly dangerous competitor.

Does the ecompetitor have a possibility of channel conflict?

Channel conflict. No, it's not a battle between England and France. In ebusiness, it's a common occurrence.

One of the advantages of ebusiness is that it wrings inefficiency out of the process of commerce. In industries where there are intermediaries adding little value, such as in industrial supplies, insurance, and books, the ebusiness function enables the subrogation of various steps in the physical distribution process, causing certain parts of the system to become superfluous.

But those parts of the distribution process will not go quietly. In situations where manufacturers are circumventing wholesalers and retailers by going direct to the customer through an ebusiness effort, those intermediaries are getting uppity and downright ornery.

Your job as a competitive intelligence analyst is to define which of your competitors is most likely to be affected by channel conflict. To find this type of weakness, you must look for competitors who provide value to the distribution process by overcoming the restrictions of space and/or time. This does not necessarily mean ecompetitors. There are certainly brick & mortar competitors that bring this value to the table. Consider any large retailer that has many stores. Because they cover so much territory, and draw customers from such a large area within each store's territory, this type of competitor actually does mitigate the problem of space for all of their suppliers. So, you don't necessarily need a Web site to mitigate that space problem. You just need reach.

This search for space and time mitigation should mean to the competitive intelligence analyst that distributors or sales personnel placed for distant representation of their principals are elements that could be vulnerable, ripe for substitution by an ebusiness system. The Web can supplant their existence unless they truly have a ubiquitous presence. Physical competitors who represent their principals so as to offer customer convenience via a 24 x 7 physical access are also ripe to be picked off by ebusiness competition whose less labor intensive operation also knows no time boundary.

Value propositions based on the mitigation of time and space restrictions are bound to change, rapidly, and it is to those that the competitive intelligence analyst must attend. Through early identification of a competitor's weakness in this area the analyst will be in a position to help draft a strategy that can exploit that weakness to advantage.

Perhaps, though, your competitor is not an intermediary that might get pushed out by channel conflict, but instead is a principal who is doing the pushing. In that case, you'll need to look at them at little differently.

Such an ecompetitor likely does not wish to alienate its entire distribution channel, at least not all at once. Instead of meeting this problem head-on, your competitor wishing to become an ecompetitor may avoid conflict by going directly to customers with an offering that is not in the current physical distribution channel. That is to say, they'll create a new product or service which will be distributed exclusively through ebusiness avenues. By doing so, they avoid conflict with distributors carrying the old line of products.

So, the competitive intelligence analyst should keep a sharp eye out for this channel conflict preemptive move. An ecompetitor that pulls this off is certainly clever and cute.

Does the ecompetitor have executive vision?

To run an ebusiness requires courage, faith, chutzpah, nerve, and the ability to see the future. Returns for the right ebusinesses will come, but they may be elusive and exist only at some point in the future. Executives running ebusinesses need vision in order to see that future and then move their companies toward that goal.

Dot coms are usually filled with this type of executive. They have plenty of vision. That's about the only thing that's keeping them going. So, if you're up against a dot com pure play, this question should not be a large issue in your competitive analysis.

If you're up against a click & mortar, however, this question raises a legitimate issue. Dot com executives are in it because they know the future will arrive, either in the form of a business model that throws off excellent profits, an IPO that skyrockets, or a lucrative buy-out by a well heeled corporate raider. Please note that they're not always right. But click & mortar executives are often in the ebusiness game "Because our competition is there." This is sometimes a good reason, but often it is not. Click & mortar guys and gals, being from a physical world company background, are often conflicted. Just like Christensen's "good managers," they may feel that they've got to produce the return, so they start acting conservatively until they discover doing so is suicide. But the competitive intelligence analyst should not automatically assume that their click & mortar competitor is run by a bunch of in-the-closet offline people, trying to put in a half-hearted appearance on the Internet.

The analyst has got to get in, roll up his or her sleeves, and research the background of the click & mortar executive as well as the person leading the pure play. Look at what they have done before. Was their previous experience in physical world business in managing something that was started by someone else, without making many, if any, incremental changes? Or, was the physical world business experience in starting a new company, division, or subsidiary? Freedom at point zero? If the target of your investigation has that type of experience, then they will fit right in at either a pure play or at a click & mortar. Then your seemingly benign executive disguised within a click & mortar could be a dangerous son-of-a-gun.

*   *   *

Financial

Does the ecompetitor choose an advantageous tax location?

Income taxes are an important part of doing business, especially for the governments that collect them. They're always there to stick their greedy little mitts out in front of you and make you cough up your "fair" share. Income taxes can claim a significant portion of any company's before tax profit. Naturally all companies attempt to minimize their income taxes so as to create a larger after-tax profit margin. Imagine what the complete elimination of income taxes could do for a profit margin.

Because of tax advantages that exist, the American competitive intelligence analyst must be alert to ecompetitors who take their operation offshore, out of the United States. There are programs set up by foreign governments, which consist of an almost turnkey ebusiness operation sweetened with the allure of no income tax. Yes. You read that correctly. No income tax.

Places like Anguilla have created complete programs for ebusinesses, specifically ebusinesses from the United States, consisting of corporate entity, office space, computer hardware, Internet connections, and other essential supplies and equipment for the budding ebusiness. All in a turnkey format. Now of course, tax advantages not withstanding, there is already enough incentive for American ebusinesspeople to locate their operations in these tropical paradises. But these governments go one step further than the beckoning of the tropical weather. They eliminate income taxes. Their reasoning is sound.

eBusinesses locating their operations in these tax havens not only purchase goods and services locally, but also hire some local labor. All of this stimulates the local economy and produces tax revenue in the form of sales and excise taxes, as well as the income taxes paid by the locals working in the ebusiness and the suppliers selling to the ebusiness. The idea for this is not new. It represents one end of the spectrum of basic fiscal policy practiced by most governments on the face of this planet.

In the 1960s, the United States government did a similar thing by offering tax advantages to companies that would locate factories in Puerto Rico, stimulating economic growth in that American protectorate. During the 1980s in the United States we referred to this practice as supply side economics and it gave birth to an economic recovery and boom which continues to this day.

So the ebusiness competitive intelligence analyst must endeavor to identify which of its competitors take advantage of these tax havens. Such ecompetitors will have an uncommon profit advantage, with all of the financial advantage that implies. This advantage contributes to their level of danger.

"The hardest thing to understand in the world is the income tax."—Albert Einstein

How is the competitor's capital structure weighted? Debt or equity heavy?

The finances of an ecompetitor are an important issue at which the competitive intelligence analyst should look. Since most dot com pure plays are start-ups, their financing is often heavily dependent upon venture capital or "angel" backed equity plays.

The competitive intelligence analyst must keep in mind that dot com start-ups are highly speculative and thus risky. They hang their hat on the hope that they will be able to continue to use their accelerating stock value as currency with which to finance operations and to attract personnel.

If your dot com competitor is a pure play and public, you will be able to secure easily the information that you need in order to conduct a financial competitive sensitivity analysis. Check their balance sheet. What is their debt to equity ratio? Do they even have any debt worth mentioning? Many will not, and believe it or not these will be the dot com pure plays who may exhibit competitive problems in the future. Take this as an example.

You're a competitive intelligence analyst for a brick & mortar company. Your company is putting together an Internet effort, but one of the things you need to know before the Internet effort proceeds is the competitive abilities of dot com pure plays already in your marketspace. You visit SEC.gov, identify dot com pure plays in your space, and start downloading the financials.

After you have done a qualitative analysis separating serious competitors from lesser threats, you begin to look at the balance sheets of the serious contenders. Very low debt to equity is what you'll most likely find, with a cash position experiencing a burn rate like that of the sun. Guess what? If your company has a significantly higher debt to equity ratio, then your company probably has a better chance of battling long term in the marketplace. This is true, of course, provided your debt to equity ratio does not force your company into a situation where your average cost of capital exceeds the returns of your business. How can such a situation be? You thought debt was a no-no.

Debt is not necessarily a bad thing. Only "too much" debt is a bad thing. The problem with equity financed competitors is that they depend on an accelerating stock value to drive everything. When Internet IPOs are issued, the underwriter and the company may intentionally hold back a large amount of stock. This is done to: 1) keep supply low on the IPO and drive the market price higher; and, 2) have more stock to issue later at, hopefully, the higher market price to which it has been driven after the IPO. As previously mentioned, they want to use the stock as currency later in the operation. In a market segment where dot coms proliferate and competition is heavy, this situation is likely to be fatal. Why? Because when the market smartens up (as we saw a la the NASDAQ in early 2000), investors realize that competition is heavy which will decrease future growth and revenue, depressing stock price accordingly.

This depression removes the ecompetitor's ability to use future stock price as currency, with which to woo future employees and purchase needed services after that stock is converted to cash. The remaining cash is then burned at an even higher rate than before. Then the ecompetitor gets caught cash short. You know the rest.

So, no matter if you work for brick & mortar or for a dot com, don't forget to analyze and forecast the competitor's financial condition. It might be the key you seek and that competitor may look a little less dangerous after you examine the debt to equity relationship.

Does the ecompetitor offer stock options or reverse options to employees?

It used to be standard procedure for an ebusiness effort, primarily a pure play, to offer stock options to its employees. Since the "crash" of the tech stock market back in Spring 2000, this tactic is now used far less. Yet now with many ebusiness efforts being developed within the walls of a physical world company (click & mortar), the idea can still apply. The click & mortar could waive the stock options of its physical world parent at the would-be ebusiness employee, trying to entice these people into their lair. The idea behind this financial temptation is this.

After a specific period of employment, the vesting period, the ebusiness awards the option to the employee to purchase the company's stock at some low price, let's say $5. If an employee has the chance to get a piece of stock at $5 and the stock's market value has risen to some insane price, say $105, the employee can exercise the option and then sell, making a cool $100 in the process. Imagine this profit multiplied over many hundreds of shares. If they exercise and sell within one year, then they pay their normal income tax rate, or about half of the value of the margin made. To reduce their tax they can always capture the 20% capital gains rate by exercising and selling after one year, but that kind of move gets into a lot of hairy tax issues like alternative minimum tax versus capital gains. Let's just keep it simple and assume the employee cashes in immediately after exercising the option.

So, the ecompetitor, if a public entity, could offer these options to employees to get them to sign on or continue employment. This is a nifty little scheme that ecompetitors can apply to get good talent. Talent that is very important in New Economy battles. This plan can make employees rich, quickly. But this plan can only work if the stock value is appreciating. Of course, other than shorting a stock, how many other plans work for a stock that is depreciating? The competitive intelligence analyst should be alert for ecompetitors offering stock option plans. The analyst should also be alert for ecompetitors offering a new variation on the standard stock option plan. This variation is called reverse stock options.

Instead of the employee waiting for the vesting period to conclude, the employee is awarded options that vest immediately. The employee may exercise those options at any time, but the stock purchased through those options will not vest for a specific time period, usually about three years. After the stock vesting period, the employee may cash them in. When this is done, the employee is not taxed at the regular income tax rate, but because the shares have been held over one year they are taxed at the lower capital gains rate of 20%, far below any regular income tax rate that an ebusiness employee would pay.

The reverse option method is a competitive tool offered by many ebusinesses as a way for the employee to decrease income taxes and maximize wealth. Such a method beats hands down the standard options method which, after waiting a vesting period of about three years, usually require a 39.6% federal income tax payment from employees, not to mention any state income tax payment. The reverse option method effectively cuts the employee's tax bill in about half. Using reverse options as a method of employee attraction and retention makes the ecompetitor highly dangerous to the analyst's company.

THE FINISH

So here we are at the end of the book.

I have presented many ideas for you to work with, but I'm sure that you may think that I have probably given too much attention to some ideas while giving short shrift to other ideas. It also may be that I left some ideas out entirely. That's very possible as this field of ebusiness changes so quickly. To stay current you will need to do more and more reading in order to stay on top of the game in competitive analysis for ebusiness.

Dangerous Competition is not meant to be an all-encompassing compendium on how to do competitive analysis in the ebusiness age. This book was meant as a stimulus in getting you to think about some general strategic ebusiness issues which, to me at least, appear critical to conducting business as we enter the 21st century. As you go about your work, you will probably find other critical ideas, appropriate to your industry, upon which I did not touch or which require an alteration of my views. This field changes so quickly; it wouldn't surprise me. Though, even if that is the case, then I have succeeded. I have succeeded in getting you to think about these issues and puzzle them out to determine where your business life lies in the future.

Now, I would just like to say a final goodbye.

The original ending of this book was at the end of the previous section. Prior to publishing, the response from most proofreaders and critiquers was to give it more of an ending, a wrap-up, and a conclusion. They said that without such a wrap-up it just came to an abrupt and screeching halt, like a British television show. I told them that the ending was as it was because I couldn't think of a decent ending. They must have regarded that answer with some suspicion, and rightly so, because that wasn't really the truth, a truth which I was reluctant then to relate to anyone. However, I will now.

The truth was that I was sick of being involved with this book, not because I was tired of the subject matter, had said my piece, or just wanted to move on as a matter of course. I did want to move on and forget about the days that I sat at my computer writing about dangerous competition. It's not that I had anything against the content of this book. It was just the atmosphere that surrounded me while writing this book that I wanted to forget.

During the summer of 2000, I wrote most of this book with my favorite cat by my feet. She was terminally ill with pancreatic cancer, beyond treatment said two vets. As I wrote, she laid in the sunshine, losing weight, disappearing ever so slowly before my eyes. It was in between frequent trips to the vet, punctuated by phone calls to and from the same, that the chapters of this book emerged. My frustration with an imminent death during that period gave birth to a slightly different writing style, more edgy, more direct, more cogently terse. At points, I felt that I was rushing. But after review, I found that those spots were punchy and directly to the point. I decided to leave them in an effort to save the reader time. Remember the discussion of saving time? If you look closely, maybe you can recognize those points.

It is at those points that the cat was at her worst. I rushed at times because somehow, for some reason, while writing I felt compelled to finish the book before we had to send her home. But I didn't succeed. I couldn't. The Supreme Architect of the Universe had recognized one of his faithful servants and wanted her home so that she could receive her wages. Whether I had finished this book or not before that day was immaterial to the man upstairs.

Perhaps I wanted to finish the book before her departure so that I could feel like I had at least some control over something. Or, that if I finished the book before she had to leave, the book would have been alive before she was dead and as a result she would always be with me in the book. Or perhaps it was simply to keep my mind off of a similar and more painful death experienced by my mother fourteen years earlier. What the reason was really didn't matter. I didn't make my deadline. That was near the end of Summer 2000. I was crushed, losing interest in the book for almost three months.

The book remained incomplete until Thanksgiving that year when, after time had healed some of the wound, I started to think. 'Yes, I didn't finish the book during her lifetime, but does that really matter? She's no less a part of the book just because she wasn't here at its conclusion.' I chuckled and in a practical reflection thought 'She couldn't have read it anyway. But if I finish, I can, in my own mind at least, always regard the book as a tribute to her.' I turned on my PC.

It is now a week before Christmas 2000. The presidential election has been decided and dimples are once again being regarded as one of those features we see as cute on little girls and not of interest on a piece of cardboard. The finishing touches are being put on this book. The cat is gone, but of course not forgotten. But something else is gone, too.

When the research for the book began, during early 2000, the dot com market was still as hot as a poker in a branding fire. That fire changed as the year progressed. Now, that market is just kind of lukewarm. My cat, who lived for eleven years, was always faithful to her human. Contrast this to many dot coms, which never made it past three years, which were certainly not faithful to their humans. The fervency for ebusiness has taken a bit of a trip. But your takeaway should be this: Although the cat and many dot coms are gone, ebusiness is not.

Internet startups are not as popular as they once were. Though, that doesn't mean that there will be no ecompetitors. eBusiness is here to stay, probably to be employed primarily by the large corporations, the click & mortar operations spoken of previously, the ones who can secure decent financing. And because ebusiness will never leave us, just as the memory of my cat will always live on for me in this book, this book, as a general primer, should never leave you.

ABOUT THE AUTHOR

Having headed one of America's largest competitive intelligence consultancies and having operated his own ebusiness strategy consultancy, Richard Telofski writes and consults on competitive intelligence topics and ebusiness strategy issues. His consulting career began with a unit of the U.S. Department of Commerce, the Trade Adjustment Assistance Program, where as a strategic planning manager he assisted American manufacturers who were having their lunches eaten by foreign competitors. Mr. Telofski has also been a college lecturer in economics, finance, and marketing, as well as a racquetball professional. He holds a Master of Business Administration degree in Marketing from Rider University and a Bachelor of Arts degree in Mass Communication from Rutgers College.

NOTES

The Eleven Critical Concepts

Note 1—Idea from "10 Driving Principles of the New Economy" in *Business 2.0*, June 1999, p. 129

Note 2—Evans & Wurster discuss a history of disintermediation in *Blown to Bits.*

Note 3—Kevin Kelly explored this concept in *New Rules for the New Economy.*

Note 4—The idea of making customers lives easier has been explored by many, but I think most effectively in regard to the use of the Internet by Patricia Seybold in *Customers.com.*

Note 5—The subject and the title of Mc Luhan's great book.

Note 6—The subject of a chapter entitled the same in *Understanding Media: The Extensions of Man.*

Note 7—A solid idea from Stan Davis & Christopher Meyer in *Blur* and Pat Seybold in *Customers.com.*

Note 8—From "10 Driving Principles of the New Economy" in *Business 2.0*, June 1999, p. 129

Note 9—Inspired by the short article, "10 Driving Principles of the New Economy" in *Business 2.0*, June 1999, p. 129

Note 10—Larry Downes & Chunka Mui touched on this in *Unleashing the Killer App.*

Note 11—Idea from Bob Morris' article "Our Kind of Lullaby" found in *fuse*, December 2000. The National Sleep Foundation statistic was also in the same article.

Note 12—Downes & Mui from *Unleashing the Killer App*.

Note 13—Kelly discussed this idea in great detail in *New Rules for the New Economy*.

Note 14—From John Hagel III & Marc Singer in *Net Worth*.

Note 15—From *New Rules for the New Economy*.

Note 16—Kelly again.

Note 17—Kelly explores this principle in detail in *New Rules for the New Economy.*

Note 18—There are many sources that explain this concept. Kelly had an excellent explanation of this concept in *New Rules for the New Economy*. Another fine explanation may be seen in *Blown to Bits*.

Note 19—John Hagel III & Marc Singer explored this idea nicely in *Net Worth*.

Note 20—Ibid. A SUPER concept. It flipped me out. I can't wait for the first true InfoMediary. Infomediaries have also been mentioned in other New Economy business sources such as *Business 2.0*.

Note 21—Ibid. The authors go to great length in the discussion of this fascinating concept.

Note 22—Davis & Meyer discuss the relationship of fractals to economies to companies in *Blur*.

Note 23—James Gleick discusses fractals in *Chaos*.

Note 24—Ibid. One of the best concepts which I have encountered in New Economy readings.

Note 25—From a Downes & Mui discussion in *Unleashing the Killer App*.

Note 26—Evans & Wurster in *Blown to Bits*.

Note 27—Ibid.

The Issues

Note 1—Suggested from reading Rosenoer et. al. in *The Clickable Corporation*, *Customers.com*, and *Blur*.

Note 2—Davis & Meyer in *Blur* introduce and discuss the concept of an offering in detail.

Note 3—The concept of "Zero Time" was discussed in "Forget Faster or Cheaper" appearing in *Net Company*, Fall 1999. This concept is explored again later in *Dangerous Competition*.

Note 4—Ibid.

Note 5—Ibid.

Note 6—The elements of disintermediation counter-strategies are discussed in detail in *eShock* by Michael De Kare-Silver.

Note 7—Originally introduced by economist Brian Arthur, and mentioned earlier in this book, increasing returns are discussed in *Blur* and *New Rules for the New Economy*.

Note 8—The section was inspired by the discussion of the theory and structure of an economic web in *New Rules for the New Economy*.

Note 9—The trademarks are the property of their respective owners.

Note 10—Porter's book, *Competitive Strategy*, has been the quintessential guide on business strategy for the past twenty years.

Note 11—Suggested from discussions in *Opening Digital Markets* by Walid Mougayar.

Note 12—Suggested in "B2B: Let's Get Vertical," *Business 2.0*, September 1999, p. 85.

Note 13—This idea is from Clayton Christensen's book *The Innovator's Dilemma* where he discusses the management paths to be taken by organizations faced with new technology.

Note 14—In "Internet Defense Strategy: Cannibalize Yourself," *Fortune*, September 6, 1999, the author reviews Christensen's theories with regard to ebusiness.

Note 15—Explored in *Unleashing the Killer App* by Larry Downes & Chunka Mui.

Note 16—In *eShock*, Michael De Kare-Silver, explores the idea of experimenters, convenience, and value shoppers, as well as other types of shoppers. The inclusion of Gen Xers in this list is original to *Dangerous Competition*.

Note 17—Again, explored in *eShock*.

Note 18—A concept which Patricia Seybold hammers home in *Customers.com*.

Note 19—Ibid.

Note 20—A prime tenant in *Information Rules* by Carl Shapiro & Hal Varian.

Note 21—Also from *Information Rules*.

Note 22—Suggested from Porter's *Competitive Strategy* and Shapiro & Varian's *Information Rules*.

Note 23—Listed as a lock-in mechanism in *Information Rules*.

Note 24—With reference to the preceding passages, again all trademarks are the property of their respective owners.

Note 25—*The Third Wave* by Alvin Toffler.

Note 26—Seybold in *Customer.com* emphasizes the importance of a consistently branded experience.

Note 27—Inspired from thoughts in *Unleashing the Killer App*.

Note 28—Inspired from Christensen in *The Innovator's Dilemma*.

Note 29—This discussion was inspired by the article, "What Kind of Global Organization Should You Build?" in *Business 2.0*, May 2000, p. 213, authored by Mohanbir Sawhney and Sumant Mandel.

Note 30—The discussion was suggested by the article, "Are You Ready for Globalization?" in *Business 2.0*, May 2000, p. 187.

Note 31—This discussion was inspired by the article, "What Regions Should You Target?" in *Business 2.0*, May 2000, p. 201.

The idea for The Eleven Critical Concepts section was inspired from reading the blurb article "10 Driving Principles of the New Economy," the book *New Rules for the New Economy*, and its precedent article "New Rules for the New Economy: Twelve Dependable Principles for Thriving in a Turbulent World," by Kevin Kelly, which appeared in the September 1997 edition of *Wired*.

The terms "Informationalize[SM]" and that term's variants and "Semi-Analog[SM]" are service marks of Becker Intelligence, Inc.

BIBLIOGRAPHY

"10 Driving Principles of the New Economy," *Business 2.0*, June 1999, p. 129

"Are You Ready for Globalization?," *Business 2.0*, May 2000, p. 187

"B2B: Let's Get Vertical," *Business 2.0*, September 1999, p. 85

Christensen, Clayton M. *The Innovator's Dilemma*. New York: Harper Business, 2000

Davis, Stan, and Christopher Meyer. *Blur*. New York: Warner Books, 1999

De Kare-Silver, Michael. *e-shock: The Electronic Shopping Revolution: Strategies for Retailers and Manufacturers*. New York: AMA Publications, 1998

Downes, Larry, and Chunka Mui. *Unleashing the Killer App*. Boston: Harvard Business School Press, 1998

Evans, Philip and Thomas S. Wurster. *Blown to Bits*. Boston: Harvard Business School Press, 2000

"Forget Faster or Cheaper," *Net Company*, Fall 1999

Gleick, James. *Chaos: Making a New Science.* New York: Penguin Books, 1987

Hagel, John III, and Marc Singer. *Net Worth.* Boston: Harvard Business School Press, 1999

"Internet Defense Strategy: Cannibalize Yourself," *Fortune,* September 6, 1999

Kelly, Kevin. *New Rules for the New Economy.* New York: Penguin Putnam, Inc., 1998

Mc Luhan, Marshall. *Understanding Media: The Extensions of Man.* New York: Mc Graw-Hill, 1964

Mc Luhan, Marshal and Quentin Fiore. *The Medium is the Massage.* New York: Bantam Books, 1967

Mc Luhan, Marshal and Quentin Fiore. *War and Peace in the Global Village.* New York: Bantam Books, 1968

Mougayar, Walid. *Opening Digital Markets.* New York: Mc Graw-Hill, 1998

Morris, Bob. "Our Kind of Lullaby," *fuse,* December 2000 (Premiere Issue), p. 72

Porter, Michael E. *Competitive Strategy: Techniques for Analyzing Industries and Competitors.* New York: The Free Press, 1980

Rosenoer, Jonathan, Douglas Armstrong, and J. Russell Gates. *The Clickable Corporation.* New York: The Free Press, 1999

Sawhney, Mohanbir and Sumant Mandel. "What Kind of Global Organization Should You Build?," *Business 2.0*, May 2000, p. 213

Seybold, Patricia. *Customers.com*. New York: Times Books, 1998

Shapiro, Carl and Hal R. Varian. *Information Rules: A Strategic Guide to the Network Economy*. Boston: Harvard Business School Press, 1999

Toffler, Alvin. *The Third Wave*. New York: Bantam Books, 1980

"What Regions Should You Target?," *Business 2.0*, May 2000, p. 201

INDEX

24 x7, 32
affiliate, 100-101
anthropology, 33-34, 45
Arpanet, 22, 29
assessment, 51, 60, 81, 92
asymptote, 35
attention, 9, 27, 31, 42, 55, 59, 105, 118, 131
Baby Boomers, 66
bandwidth, 68, 70
brand recognition, 101-102
Brand X, 66
brands, 42-43, 48, 83, 102-103
brick & mortar, 14, 57, 64, 116-117, 123, 128-129
broadband, 87
Brudda, 94, 97
burn rate, 118, 128
business school, 9, 27, 34, 57, 143-145
cannibalize, 83-85, 140, 144
cars, 74, 76-77
channel, 64, 73, 123-124
channel conflict, 123-124
chutzpah, 124

click & mortar, 110-111, 117, 125, 129, 133
commoditization, 76, 78-80, 100, 103, 113
communication, 24-27, 42, 54, 87, 92, 135
community, 52, 55
conflict, 3, 123-124
connected, 21, 29-30, 32-33, 39, 86-87, 107, 112
connection, 36, 80, 86-87
consistency, 52-53
contact, 22, 24, 51, 53-55, 94
contractual commitments, 104
convenience, 89-91, 102-104, 124, 140
convenience shoppers, 89-90
conversion, 80, 121
cool, 24, 29, 48, 65-66, 88, 129
cost savings, 77, 90, 102-104
credit card, 95-97, 121
credit procedures, 81-82
crossmedia, 111
currency, 121, 127-128
customer service, 48, 52-53, 60, 62-64
customization, 26, 62
demographics, 45, 47

differentiation, 71, 76, 78, 80-81, 100, 104, 113

diminishing returns, 35, 38, 72

disintermediated, 70

disorder, 16

disruptive, 85

distributor, 24

doodads, 65, 68, 70

dot com, 118, 125, 127-129, 133

DSL, 52

duh, 27, 119

dynamic, 72, 112

economic web, 36-38, 71, 74-76, 139

economics, 14, 34-35, 38, 72, 74, 127, 135

EDI, 108

efficiency, 33, 69, 89, 114-115

electronic, 11, 28, 35, 40, 43, 57-58, 61-64, 68, 70, 74, 77, 86-87, 107-108, 121, 143

English, 21, 122

experimenters, 89-90, 140

exponential, 32-34, 36-37, 44, 73, 116

factories, 14, 26, 127

Fat Lady, 70

financial, 44, 46, 50, 80, 117-118, 126-127, 129

flat, 113-114, 116, 118

focus, 5, 10, 78, 80

football, 7, 12

fractals, 43, 112, 138

friction, 40-43, 115

fulfillment, 30, 40, 102, 121

functionality, 50-51, 103

Gen X, 46, 65, 67, 70

Gen Xers, 90, 140

gewgaws, 65-66, 68, 70

global, 21-22, 24, 119-120, 122-123, 141, 144-145

global village, 21-22, 24, 144

grapevine, 35-36

Great Depression, 46

growth, 15, 32-37, 44-45, 87, 115, 127-128

gut, 7

harsh, 3-4

hullo, 28

iconoclastic, 42-43

income taxes, 126, 130

increasing returns, 35-36, 38-40, 71-75, 87, 90, 100, 107-108, 110, 139

Industrial Revolution, 14

industry expertise, 81, 119-120

infomediary, 42, 138

information, 1, 4-9, 11-12, 15, 17, 25-28, 31, 33-34, 37, 41-46, 48, 53, 55, 60-63, 65, 71-73, 76-77, 86-87, 89, 93, 102, 107-108, 112-114, 116-117, 120-122, 127, 140, 145

information asymmetry, 41-44, 89, 114

informationalize, 71-73, 75, 80

interactive, 22, 24-26

interactivity, 21-22, 24, 26, 30, 112

intermediate, 1-2, 100

international, 119-122

interstitials, 111

Java, 87

jonesing, 28-29

jump, 55, 57

Kruger, 59

Latin America, 122

legacy system, 57, 61

lemmings, 56

librarians, 6-7

library, 6

linebacker, 7

loadings, 51-52

local, 23-24, 52, 74, 120, 122, 126

lock-in, 100-101, 104-105, 140

logistics, 60, 63, 70, 102, 119-120

logistics, 60, 63, 70, 102, 119-120

loyalty program, 100

macro, 112

Magilla, 45

management, 3, 5-11, 13-14, 37, 44, 48-
    50, 56, 67-68, 70, 80, 83-84, 96, 99,
    105, 113-120, 140

management, 3, 5-11, 13-14, 37, 44, 48-
    50, 56, 67-68, 70, 80, 83-84, 96, 99,
    105, 113-120, 140

manager, 5, 7, 9, 12, 135

marginal cost, 26, 28

marginal profit, 26

market research, 18, 25, 93-94

marketing, 25, 42, 50, 65, 80, 86-87, 89-
    90, 101, 110-111, 116, 118-120, 135

matter, 8, 14, 24, 26, 28, 36, 56, 61, 71,
    73, 80, 106, 118, 129, 132-133

MBA, 9-10

Mc Luhan, 21-22, 24-25, 34, 137, 144

metamediary, 42

mission, 50, 55-61, 63-64

money, 12, 33, 36, 46, 63-64, 89, 100-
    101, 109, 118, 120-122

moolah, 46

Moore's Law, 15, 17

multinational, 2

narrowband, 68, 87

NASDAQ, 17, 79, 128

navigate, 51-52

New Economy, 4, 13-15, 18, 25-26, 28,
    32-34, 39-45, 47-48, 56, 68, 75, 86,
    115, 130, 137-139, 141, 143-144

Newton-John, Olivia, 10

nitty gritty, 18

non-consumable, 33-34, 72

novices, 2

offer creation, 60

Old Economy, 14-15, 19, 25, 28, 40, 51

options, 26, 115, 129-130

order taking, 60-63

organic, 35

organism, 35, 44

organization, 5, 48, 50, 78, 80, 84, 113,
    116-117, 141, 145

output, 10, 26, 35-36

outsource, 79, 88, 90, 102

parochial, 19

personalization, 55

policies, 52, 54, 65

political budget, 44

political control, 44, 114

portals, 12

practitioners, 1

pricing, 103-104, 112-113

private data network, 58

process engineering, 79

product dependancy, 71

promotion, 91, 93, 109-111

proprietary, 61, 106-108

purchasing, 71, 79, 105, 119-120

R&D, 81

railroad, 23-24

real time, 30

risk averse, 8-9, 11, 14, 115

scarcity*****

scope, 120

sea of information, 8

search, 41-43, 52-54, 61, 103, 123

search technologies, 41-43

semi-analog, 71, 73

seminar, 3

senior management, 5

site content, 50-51

social science, 34

sociological other, 29, 33

space, 13, 21-23, 25, 51, 69-70, 77, 85, 110, 123-124, 126, 128

stock value, 127-128, 130

strategic, 5, 11-13, 17, 65-66, 69, 78, 84, 110, 113, 131, 135, 145

strategy, 6-9, 11-14, 17, 43, 50, 55, 67, 70, 78-81, 86, 95, 103-104, 119, 122, 124, 135, 139-140, 144

stupid, 15, 53, 113

subversion, 114

supervision, 67

switching costs, 101-102, 104

system, 19, 24, 28, 33, 35-37, 43-45, 57-59, 61-62, 65, 69-70, 72, 74-75, 79-80, 94, 98-99, 101-102, 105-108, 112, 114, 116, 121, 123

tax, 121, 126-127, 129-130

television, 13, 21-22, 24-25, 32, 53, 109, 131

Telstar, 21

Third Wave, 15-16, 108, 140, 145

time, 2-3, 5, 7, 10, 12, 14-15, 18-19, 22-24, 26, 28-34, 38, 43, 46-47, 51-55, 58-61, 64-65, 67, 69-70, 72, 74, 77, 80, 82, 85, 87-88, 90-92, 94, 98, 102, 106-107, 109-110, 112, 115, 121, 123-124, 130, 132-133, 139

Tiny, 7

trucks, 26, 73

trust, 43, 82-83, 101-102, 119

turtleneck, 68, 75

value, 5, 16-17, 24, 29, 37-40, 62, 68-69, 71, 73-74, 76, 82, 84, 88-91, 97, 99, 102-103, 106-108, 123-124, 127-130, 140 value chain, 16-17, 24, 68-69, 71, 97

value shoppers, 89-91, 140

viral, 86-87

virtual, 11-13, 24-25, 28, 62, 64, 73-74,
    77, 92-93, 104, 109-111, 114

warehouse, 26, 121

Web server, 72

Western Europe, 122

widget, 27, 74

wireless Web, 58

wonks, 18

World Wide Wait, 87

XML, 41, 54

Zero Time, 64-65, 139